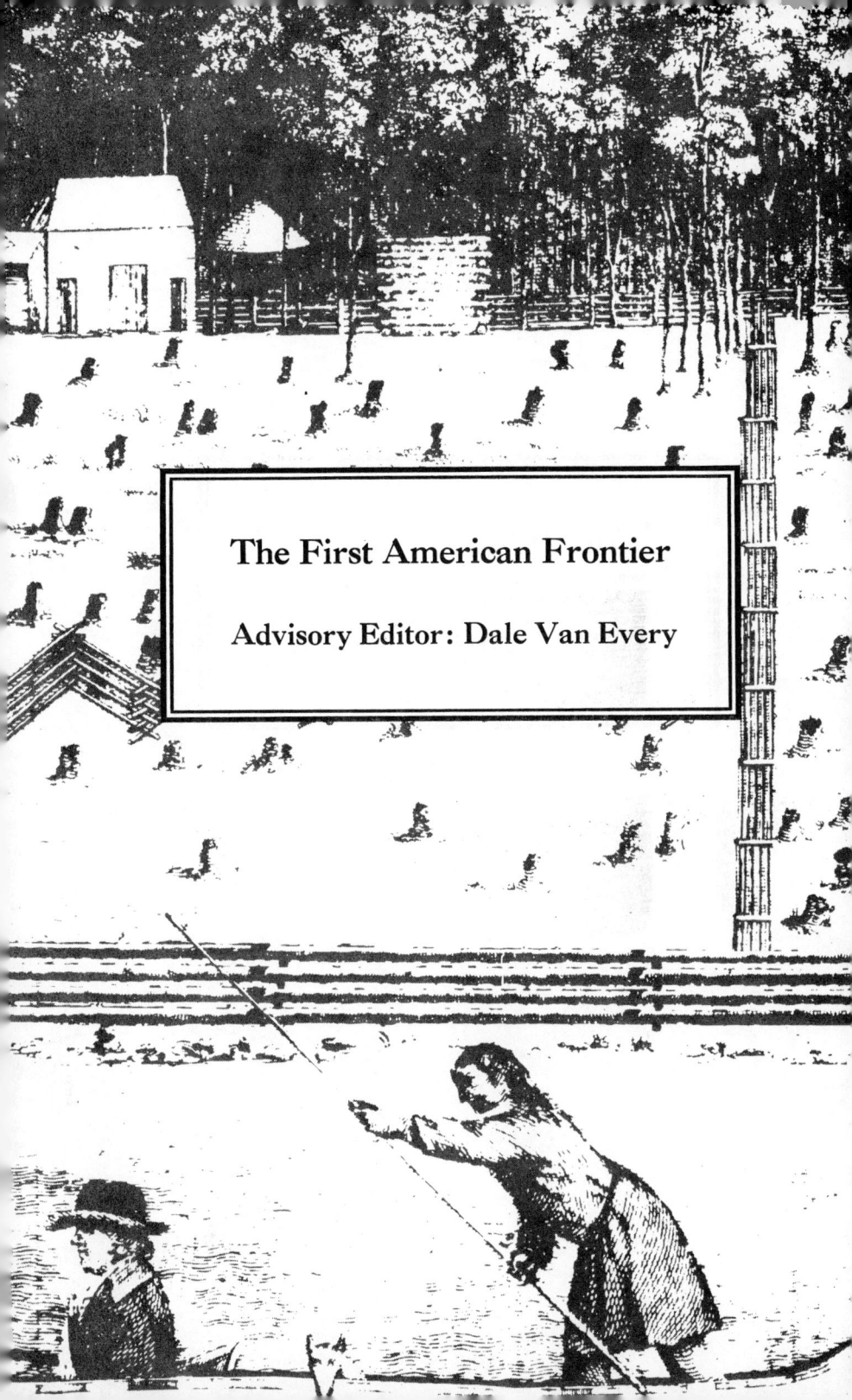

The First American Frontier

Advisory Editor: Dale Van Every

The First

American Frontier

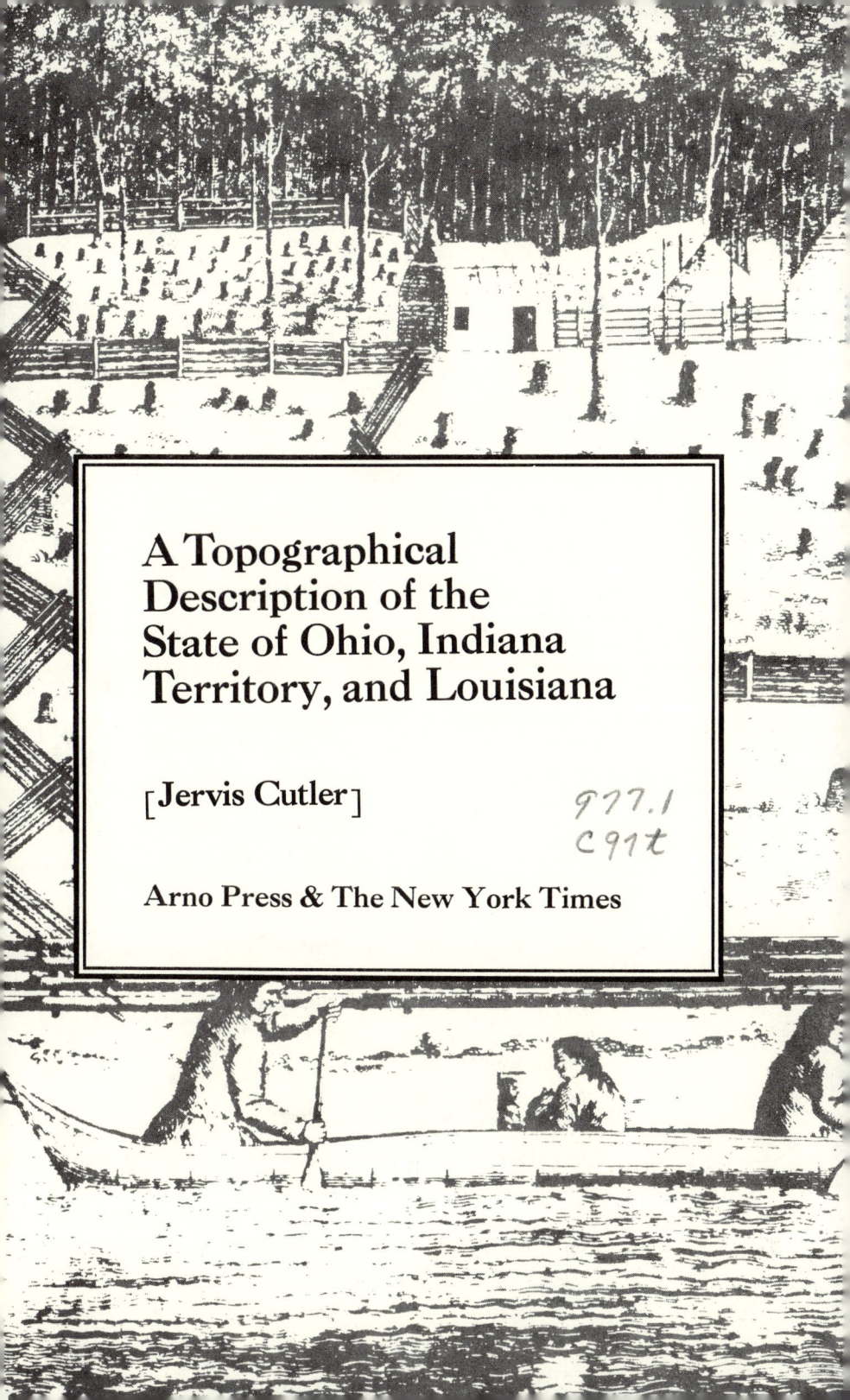

A Topographical Description of the State of Ohio, Indiana Territory, and Louisiana

[Jervis Cutler]

Arno Press & The New York Times

EG

Reprint Edition 1971 by Arno Press Inc.

Reprinted from a copy in
The State Historical Society of Wisconsin Library

LC # 78-146388
ISBN 0-405-02839-3

The First American Frontier
ISBN for complete set: 0-405-02820-2

See last pages of this volume for titles.

Manufactured in the United States of America

A

TOPOGRAPHICAL DESCRIPTION

OF THE

STATE OF OHIO,

INDIANA TERRITORY, AND

LOUISIANA.

A View of CINCINNATI on the OHIO.

A

TOPOGRAPHICAL DESCRIPTION

OF THE

STATE OF OHIO,

INDIANA TERRITORY, AND

LOUISIANA.

COMPREHENDING

THE OHIO AND MISSISSIPPI RIVERS,

AND THEIR PRINCIPAL TRIBUTARY STREAMS:

The face of the country, soils, waters, natural productions, animal, vegetable, and mineral; towns, villages, settlements and improvements:

AND

A CONCISE ACCOUNT OF THE INDIAN TRIBES WEST OF THE MISSISSIPPI.

TO WHICH IS ADDED,

AN INTERESTING JOURNAL OF MR. CHAS. LE RAYE,
While a captive with the Sioux nation, on the waters of the Missouri river.

BY A LATE OFFICER IN THE U.S. ARMY.

BOSTON:
PUBLISHED BY CHARLES WILLIAMS.
J. Belcher, Printer.
1812.

PREFACE.

THE writer of the following sheets, duing a residence in the western country for many years, has had occasion to visit several parts, to travel over a large portion of the State of Ohio, in different directions, and to descend the Ohio and Mississippi rivers, as far as New Orleans. In these excursions, opportunities continually occurred for observing, and collecting information respecting, those objects which are interesting to adventurers into a new country, and which may be gratifying to the curiosity of others. Minutes were made of the face of the country, soil, waters, natural productions, and of whatever appeared worthy of particular notice; either from his own observation, or from the information of others which he had reason to believe was authentic.

These notes were made with no other view than for his own satisfaction, and for communications to his friends. Solicitations, however, from a number of his friends, who conceived that an extract from them would be acceptable to the public, especially those interested, or who wish to become interested, in a country so rapidly increasing in population, have induced him to consent to this publication.

Information of those parts of the country which lie west of the Mississippi was collected principally from very respectable officers of the army. Several of these officers were so obliging as to favour the writer with liberty of making extracts from journals which they had kept, while marching in different parts of the country, or commanding at particular posts.

On passing with the troops from Kentucky to New Orleans, Mr. Le Raye applied to the writer for a passage with him in the boat under his immediate command. This gentleman, who is a native of Canada, had been engaged, for several years, in trading with the Indians, on the river Saskashawan, northwest of the Lake of the Woods; but, in the year 1801, he determined to turn the course of his business to the river Missouri. Unfortunately, on his first adventures he was taken captive by a band of Sioux Indians, with whom he remained more than two years and an half, before he obtained his liberty. During his captivity, he kept a journal of the most material occurrences which took place, so far as circumstances would admit. Before parting with him, he very politely presented an extract from it, with permission to make such use of it as might be thought proper. Presuming this journal will be found particularly interesting, it is annexed to this publication.

A general account of the State of Ohio, it is believed, will be acceptable to those who have lands or friends in this State, or who may contemplate emigrating there themselves. The remarks are principally confined to those, which would naturally occur to a cursory traveller, passing, in different directions, through the several countries. It is not improbable that this part of the narrative will appear the least interesting to some, but to others, it is conceived, it may be a species of information that will be desirable. In the arrangement of this publication, it was thought most eligible to begin with the State of Ohio, and proceed to the southern and western parts of the country.

A

TOPOGRAPHICAL DESCRIPTION

OF THE

STATE OF OHIO.

THE first purchase of land in the State of Ohio, after the Indian title was extinguished, was made by the Ohio company. On the 27th of November, 1787, Congress made and executed a contract with the agents of the Ohio company for the sale of one million and an half of acres, at the price of one million of dollars, to be paid for in final settlement securities. This tract, was bounded on the east by a line called the seventh range which had been previously run ; southerly on the Ohio river ; westerly on the seventeenth range of townships, and to extend so far north, that a line running east to the first boundary, should contain, exclusive of the reservations, the quantity of land contracted for.

The first regular settlement of this State commenced in the year 1789. A party of about sixty men from New-England, under the superintendence of General Rufus Putnam, and hired and paid by the company, arrived at the mouth of the Muskingum on the 7th of April, and immediately began to clear the land on the eastern side of the river. In the month of August, eight families had arrived, who inhabited the temporary buildings, erected for their accommodation, on that pleasent and commanding situation where the beautiful and thriving town of Marietta now stands. In the course of the autumn more arrived, so that, at the beginning of June, 1790, there were twenty families on the ground.

It was the intention of this company, among whom were many of the officers of the revolutionary army, to have made a rapid settlement, but the Indians beginning to commit depredations, checked the emigration from the Atlantic States. In the winter of 1791, several persons in the out settlements were killed, and others taken prisoners. The people were obliged to erect posts of defence at Bellepre and at Wolf Creek. Marietta was strongly stockaded, and the inhabitants lived in a garrison state, until after the victory gained by General Wayne, on the 20th of August, 1794.

Soon after the Ohio company had made this purchase, another contract was made with Congress by Col. John C. Symmes, for a tract of land supposed to contain about one million of acres, lying within the following limits: beginning at the mouth of the Great Miami river, and thence running up the Ohio to the mouth of the

Little Miami river; thence up the main stream of the Little Miami to the place where a due west line, to be continued from the western termination of the northern boundary line of the grant made to the Ohio company, shall intersect the said Little Miami river; thence due west, continuing the said western line to the Great Miami river; thence down the Great Miami to the place of beginning.

Settlements commenced in the autumn of 1789, on this tract, under the direction of Col. Symmes, principally by emigrations from the State of New Jersey. But the settlers here were subjected to embarrassment similar to those of the Ohio company, in consequence of the Indian war. The settlement made little progress until after the conquest of General Wayne, and the treaty with the Indians, in the succeeding year.

Not long after the commencement of these settlements, another of considerable magnitude was begun, on a tract of land, called the Connecticut Reservation, situated on the northeast corner of the State, and bounded east by the Pennsylvania line, on the north by lake Erie, and extending westward as far as Sandusky lake. These settlers came principally from the State of Connecticut.

These were the first settlements undertaken on a large scale, within the limits of the State of Ohio, but made little progress until after the close of the Indian war.

Another very considerable settlement commenced, in 1796, on a tract of land, called the Virginia Reservation, situated between the Scioto and Little Miami rivers. This land was located by army warrants, granted originally to the troops of the Virginia line of the revolutionary army. A part of the settlers were from Virginia, but far the greatest number from the State of Kentucky. The town of Chillicothe was began in the autumn of this year (1796), and so rapid was the increase of inhabitants that it was made an incorporate town in about five years. The Territorial Assembly of the representatives of the people convened in this town for several years, and it continued the seat of government until 1809, when, by act of Assembly, it was moved to Zanesville on the river Muskingum.

On the 13th of April, 1802, the people were authorized, by an act of Congress, to form a constitution and State government, and were accordingly admitted into the Union upon the same footing with the original States. By the same act, the boundaries of the State were established on the following lines, viz. "Beginning on the east by the Pennsylvania line; on the south, by the Ohio river to the mouth of the Great Miami river; on the west by a line drawn due north from the mouth of the Great Miami, and on the north by an east and west line drawn through the southerly extremes of lake Michigan, running east, after intersecting the due north line aforesaid, from the north of the Great Miami, until it shall intersect lake Erie, or the territorial line, and thence with the same through lake Erie, to the Pennsylvania line aforesaid."

The number of inhabitants, since the peace with the Indians, in 1795, has been rapidly increasing. In 1803, it appeared that there were 15,314 white males of 21 years of age and upwards. Calculating on this *data*, it has been supposed, that the whole number of inhabitants at that time could not be less than 76,000. It has been presumed that the emigrants coming into the State annually, for several years, were about 12,000. The embarrassment, however, occasioned by the embargo, operated as a very serious check on the acquisition of inhabitants from the other States, as well as from foreign nations. The present number within the State, cannot with much certainty be ascertained. By a late estimation, from the probable natural increase, and the additions by emigration, the population is stated, in round numbers, to be 200,000. The accuracy of this estimation will soon be decided by the next census.*

Having traversed a large portion of the State in several directions, it will be attempted to give a

* By the census taken in 1810, the number of inhabitants are 230,843.

cursory description of the face of the country, soils, and the natural and cultivated productions, beginning at the eastern boundary.

Near the mouth of the Little Beaver Creek the boundary line between the States of Pennsylvania and Ohio, meets the Ohio river, 42 miles below Pittsburgh. Near the creek are some rich bottoms or intervals, but the land back rises into high hills; on some of them is a good soil and capable of cultivation. There are some handsome farms, producing wheat, rye, barley, oats, flax, hemp and Indian corn. Not far from the mouth of the Little Beaver, a spring has been found, said to rise from the bottom of the river, from which issues an oil which is highly inflammable, and is called *Seneca oil.* It resembles *Barbadoes tar*, and is used as a remedy for rheumatic pains. People who have travelled for several days on foot, have found much relief by rubbing this oil over their joints.

The land from the Little Beaver to the Muskingum, on the Ohio, ascends into high hills, some of them terminating in elevated peaks, but there are frequently, large rich vallies that intervene, at the base of the hills. Towards the Muskingum the summits of the hills become more broad and fleet. Some of them are free of rocks, and having a rich soil admit of cultivation. The greater part of these hills may be profitably improved for orchards and grazing of sheep and cattle. As far as

Wheeling and Grave Creek they abound with coals, and generally of a good quality.

In many of these hills are quarries of excellent free stone, capable of a good polish, and make beautiful walls in buildings. Some of these stones, when first taken out of the ground, are so soft that they can be worked into various forms with carpenter's tools. On the side of a hill above Steubenville, it is said, there is a spot of ground, that when covered with a considerable depth of snow, a smoke is seen to rise from it, as if it were heated by a subterranean fire. And that near the base of the same hill, if an hot sun succeeds a shower of rain, an excellent white, fine salt may be collected from the surface of the rocks. Not far from Georgetown, 38 miles below Pittsburgh, it is said, a gold mine has lately been discovered. A specimen, it is reported, has been tried by a silver-smith at Pittsburgh, who declared it to be pure gold, without alloy. The lump had the appearance of being found in running water.

The base of some of the hills extends to the bank of the river, others recede leaving wide bottoms of a very rich and deep soil. When the hills approach the river on one side, they usually recede from it, on the other, so that there are wide bottoms, alternately, on both sides the river. Much of the soil in these bottoms, especially the first, (for there are two and three bottoms rising one above the other, forming a sort of glacis) has been found as deep as the bed of the river. The hills are clothed with a thick forest of trees, consisting of white, red and black oak, hickory, ash, chestnut, poplar, sassafras, dogwood, and the grape vine. The bottoms are covered with a heavy growth. The largest trees are button-wood, called here sycamore, elm, black walnut, tulip tree, and beach. The smaller trees consist of hickory, white walnut or butter-nut, locust, honey-locust, buck eye, mulberry, sugar-maple, cherry tree, crab-apple tree, plumb tree, papaw, and willow. The grape vine abounds on the bottoms, and grows to a prodigious size, ascending to the tops of the loftiest trees. The passenger, gliding down the river in the summer, is amused and delighted with the appearance of these vines on the upper branches and tops of the trees, forming large canopies, festoons, arbours, grottoes, with numerous other fantastic figures. Some of the trunks of these vines are of a size which will admit them to be split into four rails for fence.

The sugar-maple is a tree of immense value to the people of this State. It ought to be a first object with every man, when he begins to cultivate his land, as much as possible, to preserve these trees. Each tree, from eighteen to twenty inches in diameter, will yield four pounds of sugar every season. The process of making is to tap the tree with an auger, drive into the hole a wooden tube, and place a trough under it to receive the water. Large kettles being placed in the most convenient situation among the trees, and a fire made under them, the water is brought in buckets, where it is moderately boiled, until it comes to a consistency which scarcely admits of any longer stirring with a stick made for that purpose. It is then removed from the kettle, and is still constantly stirred until it is cold. As it cools it granulates and becomes bright and dry. The grain of this sugar, made at the beginning of the season, very much resembles the sugar made in Louisiana from the sugar cane, and not inferior to the best Musquevado. The quality of the sugar depends much on care and cleanliness in making of it. The season for making, and the time it continues, varies according to the state of the weather. It generally commences in February and continues about six weeks. When the trees are at a distance from the house, a camp is formed in a central place among the trees, and is called the *sugar camp*. The whole family sometimes resorts to this camp, and women and children assist in making the sugar. In camps consisting of one hundred and fifty to two hundred trees, have been made from five hundred to a thousand pounds of sugar, in one season. An average price of the sugar may be about ten cents per pound. Sugar has been made late in autumn, after frosts or falls of snow, but it depends on the weather.

The land back from the Ohio is best for farms. The hills diminish in height and size, and though interspersed with ridges and swelling hills, a large portion of the ground is sufficiently level for all the purposes of cultivation. Much of the land on hills and ridges is arable, and admits of easy tillage, having a rich and deep soil; and most of the ridgy and rough lands may be made useful for grazing and orchards. From the eastern boundary to the river Scioto, the same growth of trees and shrubs which have been mentioned generally prevail; although the different kinds grow more plentifully on some lands, than they do on others, and in several places there are considerable growths of pine. In the tract of land called the seven ranges there are some hills and ridges which are high and form steep precipices. In this kind of land the soil is thin, and growth small, consisting of oak and hickory, the summits of the hills tufted with pine. On the seven ranges there are few inhabitants, excepting near the Ohio. These people are principally emigrants from Pennsylvania.

The great road from Cumberland on the Potomac river, commonly called the United States road, crosses the Ohio at Wheeling, where there is a distributing post-office, that receives and despatches the mail once a week to the westward, and twice a week to the eastward. Where this road leaves the Ohio it takes a westerly direction, and passes through the State of Ohio to Limestone, in Kentucky. This road is the great thorough fare of people, in which there is incessant travelling from different parts to the Atlantic States, and from these States into the western country. The land through which the road passes from the Ohio to Zanesville, on the Muskingum, is uneven, but rich, pretty thickly settled and well cultivated. There are four thriving villages. St. Clairsville is the largest, containing a number of handsome houses and several stores of goods. It is the principal town in the county of Belmont.

Passing down the Ohio from Wheeling to Muskingum, there are only scattering settlements on the rich lands near the river.

The town of Marietta, situated at the confluence of the Muskingum with the Ohio, has greatly increased in population and wealth. Before the settlement commenced, the ground on the eastern side of the Muskingum was laid out in the form of a city, containing one thousand lots of 90 feet front and 180 feet rear. The squares were oblong, separated by spacious streets, which intersect at right angles. A large square was reserved for a market, and several others, in different parts of the city, for public uses, or pleasure ground. There are now, on the city ground, more than one hundred houses, and about one sixth part are built with brick and stone. Many of the houses are large and

2*

built in a handsome style. The form in which the town is built, adds much to its elegance, and the gentle rising of the city ground back from the Ohio, affords an extended and delightful prospect of the rivers and distant hills, which is greatly heightened and enlivened by the shipping and various kinds of water craft floating on the streams. A part of the town is built on the opposite side of the Muskingum, and the houses not inferior in elegance to those on the city ground.

Marietta is the seat of justice for the county of Washington, and has a court-house and jail. There are two religious societies; the largest is Congregational, who have erected a handsome meeting-house. It has an academy, which is also improved as a house for public worship.

Within the area of the ground laid out for a city, at the northeast part of it, are a number of the ancient works so frequently found in the western country. They consist principally of two large oblong squares and an elevated mound, in the form of a cone. The largest square contains forty acres, and the smallest twenty. They are enclosed by walls or ramparts of earth, without any ditches, from six to ten feet in height, and about thirty feet in breadth at the base, with twelve openings, or gate-ways, at regular distances from each other. From one of the angles of the largest square nearest the Muskingum, is the appearance of the walls of a *covert way*, leading towards the river. The highest part of the remains of these walls is twenty-one feet, and forty feet in breadth at the base. The mound of earth, in form of a sugar-loaf, is thirty feet in height, and the base 115 feet in diameter. It is situated at a little distance from the smallest square. These works were included in public squares and have been carefully preserved; but a small opening has been made in the conic mound and found to contain human bones. Although these ancient works fill the beholder with astonishment, others have been discovered of far greater magnitude. On a branch of the Muskingum, about ninety miles from Marietta, there are these ancient works extending about two miles in length, and the ramparts and mounds of a much greater height than those found here. Vestiges of ancient works, of different forms and sizes, and at small distances, are to be found over the whole State, and in many other parts of the western country.

Marietta is favourably situated for commerce and manufactories. The depth and gentle motion of the water, in the mouth of the Muskingum, and the cheapness of excellent ship timber, render this one of the best places for ship-building on the Ohio river. A number of large ships and brigs were built in a short time, and the employment was rapidly progressing until a stop was put to it by the embargo. Three rope walks, of nearly a thousand feet in length, were erected, and the numerous mechanic branches, connected with the highly important employment of ship-building were established. The Muskingum (which means, in the Indian language *Elk's Eye*) is of immense importance to this town. The current is moderate, rarely overflowing its banks, and may be navigated with keel boats and other craft, during the summer, as far as Zanesville, sixty miles from Marietta. There are falls, but happily formed for erecting water works of every description. Above the falls the river is again navigable, not only in the main stream, but many of the numerous branches which meander through a rich and level country in their way to the river. The largest branch is the Tuskarawa, which, with only a portage of seven miles and an half, communicates with the Cayahoga river, emptying into lake Erie. The immense quantity of produce which this fertile tract of country is capable of yielding for market, and the easy transportation, cannot fail of rendering Marietta a convenient place of sale or deposit, from whence, by the ships built here, it may be sent abroad. Materials for many different manufactories may be procured here with so much facility, and from the well known spirit of industry and enterprize prevailing among the people, there can be no doubt of their entablishment in process of time. A bank was established here in 1807, with a deposit of an 100,000 dollars, from which essential benefits have been derived. There is a post-office, two printing offices, and two weekly papers.

Ascending the Muskingum from Marietta, at the distance of five miles, is Captain Devol's ship-yard, where a number of large vessels have been built, and one of them more than 200 tons. The workmanship and timber of these vessels are said not to be inferior to any that have been built in the United States. Their frames were black walnut, which is said to be as durable as the live oak and is much lighter. The plank of these vessels are said to be of an unusual length and firmness. The forests here abound with the best of timber, such as white oak, black walnut and locust, and the prodigious height and size of the trees, admit of the selection of any dimensions which can be wanted. Excellent masts of yellow pine are easily procured. Iron-ore is found, in places, in almost every part of the State, and a sufficiency of bar iron can be obtained without difficulty. But the want of a greater number of furnaces and forges, keeps up the price higher than it otherwise would be. As much tar as can be wanted is brought down the Alleghany river. The people can, with ease, raise as much hemp and flax as would be sufficient to supply the whole of the United States.

The lands on the Muskingum above Marietta are rich, thickly settled and well cultivated. At the distance of twelve miles is the town of Adams, and twenty-three miles, by water, is the town of Waterford, within the purchase of the Ohio company. At a small distance above this purchase, the bottom lands are narrow, and the hills are many of them steep, tufted with pine, for about thirty miles. They then begin to recede from the river, and bottoms increase in width to Zanesville; at the distance of a few miles west of the river the face of the country is swelling hills, with a rich soil, and the growth principally beach and oak.

The hills on this river abound with coal, and much of it of an excellent quality. It is said a vein of coal has been found crossing the bed of the river, remarkable for its purity. The pieces of the coal have the appearance of varnish, somewhat resembling japan, and when laid on the fire, a kind of fusion is produced, which continues until it is consumed by evaporation, without disagreeable smell, and deposits scarcely any cinder or ashes. Coal has been sold at Marietta at about three cents the bushel, and is much used by the inhabitants for fuel, in preference to wood, when wood can be purchased at one dollar per cord.

Descending the Ohio, at the distance of ten miles below Marietta is Bellepre. This beautiful village is several miles in length, extending to the Little Hockhocking river. The people are principally farmers. The good management and excellent culture of their farms has been much admired. An early attention was paid to raising different kinds of fruit trees. Orchards of apple trees of large extent have been planted, which are now become extremely productive. The fruit is of various kinds and of the best flavour. Prodigious quantities of cider is made, and when the fruit is properly collected and carefully made, the liquor is of the first quality. They have likewise large peach orchards for making peach brandy. In this part of the State apple trees and all garden fruit trees thrive surprisingly, and the flavour and size of the fruit is considered superior to that of the Atlantic States. The gardens yield all the culinary plants in high perfection. The various sorts of melons are delicious and grow to a large size.

Opposite to Bellepre is the beautiful island owned by Mr. Blannerhasset. The name of this unfortunate man, whom Col. Burr, by his artifice seduced to engage in his nefarious schemes, is well known. This may render some description of this delightful seat the more interesting. The following was written by a gentleman, on a tour from Philadelphia, and published in the Ohio Navigator.

"*Blannerhasset's Island.*—On ascending the bank from the landing, (a quarter of a mile below the eastern end) we entered at a handsome double gate, with hewn stone square pilasters, a gravel walk, which led us about one hundred and fifty paces to the house, with a meadow on the left, and a shrubbery on the right, separated by a low hedge of privy-sally, through which innumerable columbines and various other hardy flowers were displaying themselves to the sun. The house is built of wood, and occupies a square of about fifty-four feet each side, is two stories high, and in just proportion; it is connected with two wings, by a semicircular portico, or corridor running from each front corner. The shrubbery well stocked with flowering shrubs, and all the variety of evergreens natural to the climate, as well as several exotics, surrounded the garden, and has gravel walks labyrinth fashion winding through it. The garden is not large, but seems to have had every delicacy of fruit, vegetable and flower, which this fine climate and luxurious soil produces. In short Blannerhasset's island is a most charming retreat for any man of fortune fond of retirement, and it is a situation perhaps not exceeded for beauty in the world. It wants however the variety of mountain, precipice, cataract, distant prospect, &c. which constitute the grand and sublime."

From Bellepre to the Great Hockhocking the country is uneven, and some high hills near the Ohio, but the soil is generally good and the growth is large. Excellent farms are made back from the Ohio on both the Hockhockings, and on their branches where there are large bottoms, and rich swelling hills.

On the Great Hockhocking thirty miles from the Ohio, are the two college townships granted by Congress to the Ohio company for the endowment of a University. Athens, one of these townships, is beautifully situated on a bend of the river, commanding an extensive prospect. The settlements commenced in 1797. The town is laid out in a regular form; the never failing springs of excellent water are numerous; and the soil extremely rich and fertile. The number of families in the town supposed to be about one hundred. An act incorporating the university was granted in 1801. A building has been erected for the instruction of youth, who are at present under the care of a preceptor. The bottom lands on this river are more extensive and of a better quality than those on the Muskingum.

On this river thirty miles from Athens and five miles beyond the line of the Ohio company's purchase, are falls commodiously situated for any kind of water works. The descent of the water is nine feet, and the stream never fails at any season of the year. Above the falls, the land on both sides the river, is level and rich. There the hills flatten off into extensive plains.

From the great Hockhocking, or the Ohio, to Galliopolis, and from thence to the mouth of the Scioto river, the land is hilly, clothed with an heavy growth of excellent wood and useful timber, but interspersed with rich bottoms and intervals. Receding from the Ohio the hills and ridges diminish, until the land becomes sufficiently level for all the purposes of culture. Where settlements have been made in this hilly land, the farms are very productive, and it is considered as the best land in the State for orcharding.

On Shade river, ten or twelve miles below the Great Hockhocking, handsome, flourishing settlements have commenced. Opposite the mouth of the great Kanhawa is Fairhaven, a small, but beautiful village, most delightfully situated.

Three miles below is Golliopolis situated on the high bank of the Ohio. It was began in the year 1792, and was settled by about five hundred French people, emigrants directly from France who erected about an hundred houses.

These people, wholly unacquainted with clearing up forests of heavy timber, after forming handsome gardens, and planting vineyards and orchards, became discouraged. Finding themselves in hazard by the Indian war, they began to desert the town. Some went down the river about twenty-five miles and settled on donation lands given them by Congress, opposite little Sandy creek, but many of them went down the Mississippi to Louisiana. The town has since been on the decline. It is the seat of justice for the county of Gallia. Before these people left Galliopolis they made a considerable quantity of wine, mostly from the native grape. Some of the wine made here, when improved by age, is said to have been of an excellent quality.

From Galliopolis to the mouth of the Great Scioto are few settlements, excepting the new French settlement: on a tract of 20,000 acres given by Congress to the original French settlers at Galliopolis. This tract extends eight miles on the Ohio river, and is situated nearly opposite the Little Sandy river. Adjoining this land is a grant of 4000 acres, made to Man. Gervis, who has laid out a town upon it, to which he has given the name of Burrsburgh.

Above the mouth of the Great Scioto is the town of Portsmouth and below it the town of Alexandria, both of which are favourably situated for becoming places of much business. The Scioto is a large and beautiful river. When overflowed, the waters extend but a small distance from its natural banks. Both sides are bordered with rich bottoms and a great extent of excellent land for culture. It is navigable for keel boats to a great distance, and for small craft to a portage within four miles of Sundusky lake.

Having gone down the Ohio to the Scioto river, we will now return to Zanesville, on the Muskingum, and on the great road leading from Wheeling to Limestone, in Kentucky. Zanesville is situated on the east bank of the Muskingum, about eighty-five miles by water from

Marietta. Congress, in 1796, made a grant of this tract of land to Ebenezer Zane, as a compensation for opening a road from Wheeling to Limestone, and establishing and maintaining ferries over the rivers on this route. Col. Zane laid out this town in 1800. Its progress was slow, and there were few houses with either brick or stone chimneys, until 1805. Since that time its improvements have been nearly equal to its local advantages. It is situated on a bend of the river opposite to the great falls, and being on elevated ground, has a variegated and commanding prospect. It contains a considerable number of large and convenient houses; and the buildings are annually increasing. The court-house is nearly completed, built with beautiful free stone and in an elegant style. The seat of the State government is now removed to this town, where it is expected it will be permanent. The post-office in this town is a distributing office, from which mails are sent off in different directions. On the west side of the river is Springfield, containing about fifty houses, and some of them handsome buildings. There are four or five stores of different kinds of goods. Here Licking Creek discharges its waters from the westward into the Muskingum, after meandering through an extensive country of the first rate lands. About four miles from the mouth of this creek is a beautiful cataract formed by a rock extending across the stream at right angles, and producing a fall of seven and an half feet, while the water above and below appears to be on a perfect level. Besides a grist and saw mill, a furnace has been erected, which was expected to go into operation the last summer. Near the furnace is the appearance of a large quantity of iron-ore, supposed to be of a superiour quality. Coal abounds in this vicinity and can be procured nearly as cheap as at Marietta.

On the State road, west of the Muskingum, are rich and moderate swelling hills. On the northern side of the road they gradually flatten off almost to a level, and are clothed with excellent timber, consisting principally of oak, hickery, beach, black walnut, blue and black ash, mulberry, elm, buckeye, cherry, and gum. The soil is deep and rich. This description of land extends from the head waters of the Muskingum, to the waters of Scioto and Miami's, and northward to Lake Erie with little variation. Only a few large hills and ridges are distributed over a great extent of country.

On the State road, 39 miles from Zanesville, is the town of New Lancaster. This town was laid out by Col. Zane, in the year 1800, on a delightful spot, and has increased with great rapidity. It is built on the east side of the Great Hockhocking, where the stream is not more than six yards in width, but on rising ground, and where a beautiful prairie or natural meadow, stretches along the bank of the river for several miles, and about half a mile in width. This prairie renders

3*

the situation of the town exceedingly pleasant and agreeable. It contains perhaps about an hundred houses, built in a very neat manner, with hewn timber, and principally on one street. It has an handsome brick court-house, four stores of goods, and four taverns. The town and the adjacent country is settled mostly with Germans, from the vicinity of Lancaster, in Pennsylvania. It is the seat of justice for the county of Fairfield.

From New-Lancaster to Chilecothe is thirty-eight miles, and the face of the country, excepting near Lancaster, where are a few moderate hills, is very much a continued plain. It has a thin soil and is badly watered. The growth small, consisting mostly of black and white oak and some hickory. The soil inclines to clay, which is considered indifferent for farming land. On the southern extremity of this glade of land commence the chains of hills which extend on the Ohio and its branches for several hundred miles. On the northern extremity of this glade, the land is very flat and low, and much of it too wet for cultivation; but where the swells are so high as not to be overflowed in the winter and spring, the soil is rich, and produces large timber. At the distance of 28 miles from Lancaster, about three miles north of the State road, the Pickawa plains begin and extend to the Scioto river. They are several miles in width, not entirely level, but interspersed with gentle swells, which render the prospect the more agreeable. This tract is destitute of trees or shrubs, excepting a few compact clusters of trees, surrounded with thick bushes, appearing like scattered islands in a bay. The soil is good, and a fine stream of water passes on the south side. They are said to produce the best wheat raised in the State. There are two small villages on them, containing about 50 houses, and a wind-mill has been erected which grinds all their grain. These plains have been considered as the handsomest tract of land in this part of the country. The land from the Pickawa plains, in a northerly direction, for thirty or forty miles is level, interspersed with wet prairies, nearly to the forks of the Scioto, and thinly settled. Near the forks the land is good and thickly settled. In an easterly direction from the forks of the Scioto to the waters of Licking Creek is a largely extended tract of level lands, with some wet prairies but mostly a very rich soil, and is fast settling. At the distance of 38 miles is the town of Granville, built by a number of emigrants principally from Granville in Connecticut, where are thirty houses, and the country well settled around it. East of Granville, about seven or eight miles, is Newark, on the waters of Licking Creek. It contains about 60 houses, a log court house and jail, and a large log Presbyterian meeting house. It is the seat of justice for Licking county. This tract of country is well settled as far east as Zanesville. The land father northward continues level, but is much of it low and swampy, and is thinly settled.

South of the State road as it approaches the Scioto, twenty-eight miles in a southeasterly direction from Chilicothe and 83 from Galliopolis on the Ohio, are the Great Scioto salt-works. The land is hilly and covered with a heavy growth of timber. The salt water is found near the banks of a stream which runs into the Scioto, and is called Salt Creek, at the depth of about twelve feet from the surface of the ground. Fresh water, as it passes over, is prevented from flittering into the salt water, by an extremely hard pan of clay. There are sixteen furnaces, and when in operation, each furnace will make 70 or 80 bushels of salt in 24 hours. The method of constructing a furnace is to dig a long trench in a hard pan of clay, four feet deep at one end and ten feet at the other, with a gradual descent into the deep end, which is the mouth of the furnace. Ninety kettles of thirty gallons each, arranged in two tiers, are placed in the trench. A fire is made at the deepest end, and a chimney is formed at the other, in a manner that will admit of a strong draught through the length of the furnace. The water is pumped by horses or mules into a large cistern, and then laded into the kettles. An intense heat is necessary for boiling the water. As the water evaporates at the mouth of the furnace, what remains in the kettles is laded into those near the chimney, and these kettles are again filled with water, so that the water near the chimney is in a constant state of crystallization. Tallow and Indian meal are used to promote the crystalization. It requires about 600 gallons of water at these works for one bushel of salt. There are no settlers near the salt-works, excepting those concerned in making salt.

Chilicothe, an Indian name, signifying *town*, is situated on the west bank of the Scioto, where the State road crosses the river. In the year 1796, Col. Nathaniel Massie, with eight or ten men, who accompanied him from Kentucky, explored the wilderness to this spot. They planted and raised Indian corn, on a rich prairie, about two miles below the town. In autumn they formed the plan and laid out the town in lots. The next spring they brought out their families and commenced the settlement. From this small beginning has risen up, in about thirteen years, one of the most beautiful towns in the western country.

The following description of the Scioto and Chilicothe is from a gentleman who made a tour into the western country, from Philadelphia, in the year 1807, and is taken from the Ohio Navigator.

" Chilicothe is most beautifully situated on the banks of the Scioto about 45 miles by land, and nearly seventy following the meanders of the river from its confluence with the Ohio, which it joins between Portsmouth and Alexandria. In all that distance the river has a gentle current and unimpeded navigation for large keels and other craft of four feet draught of water. It continues navigable for smaller boats and batteaux upwards of one hundred miles above the town towards its source to the northward, gliding gently through a natural, rich, level, and rapidly improving country. The situation of the town is on an elevated and extensive plain of nearly ten thousand acres of as fine a soil as any in America, partly in cultivation, and partly covered with its native forests. This plain is nearly surrounded by the Scioto, which turning suddenly to the northeast from its generally southerly course, leaves the town to the southward of it, and then forms a great bend to the eastward and southward. Water street which runs about east by north parallel to the Scioto, is half a mile long, and contains ninety houses. It is 84 feet wide and would be a fine street, had not the river floods caved in the bank in one place near the middle, almost into the centre of it. There is now a lottery on foot to raise money for securing the bank against any further encroachments of the river. Main street parallel to water street, one hundred feet wide, as is market street, which crosses both at right angles, and in which is the market house, a neat brick building, eighty feet long. The court house in the same street, is neatly built of free stone on an area of 45 by 42 feet, with a semicircular projection in the rear, in which is the benches of the judges. It has an octagonal belfry rising from the roof, painted white with green lettices, which is an ornament to the town, as is the small plain belfry of the Presbyterian meeting house, a handsome brick building in main street; in which street also is a small brick Methodist meeting house. These are the only places of public worship in the town, if I except the court house which is used occasionally by the Episcopalians and other sects.

" The whole number of dwelling houses, as I counted them, is two hundred and two, besides four brick, and a few framed ones now building. I reckoned only six taverns with signs, which small proportion of houses of that description speaks volumes in favour of the place. There are fourteen stores, a post-office, and two printing offices, which each issues a Gazette weekly.

" The soil of the town being of a gravelly kind, the streets are generally clean. The houses are of free stone, brick or timber clapboarded, the first of which is got in the neighbourhood, is of a whitish brown colour, and excellent for building. They are mostly very good, and are well painted. On the whole, I think Chilicothe is not exceded in beauty of plan, situation, or appearance, by any town I have seen in the western part of the United States.

" There is here a remarkable Indian monument in Mr. Winship's garden in the very heart of the town. Like that at Grave Creek, it is round at the base, about seventy or eighty feet diameter, but differs from it by being round instead of flat on the top, which has an elevation of about thirty feet perpendicular from the level of the plain. It is formed of clay, and though it has been perforated by the proprietor, nothing has been found to justify the common opinion of these mounts having been burrows or cemetries. They talk of having it levelled, as it projects a little into market street, but I think it a pity to destroy any of the very few vestiges of Aboriginal population which this country presents to the curious and inquisitive traveller.

"From a steep hill about three hundred feet perpendicular height, just outside the western extremity of the town, is a most charming view of the streets immediately below, under the eye like a plan on paper; then the Scioto from one hundred to one hundred and fifty yards wide, winding on the left, with some low hills about two miles beyond it, terminating the view to the northeast; while to the eastward and to the westward, as far as the eye can reach both ways, is spread a country partly flat, and partly rising in gentle swells, which, if cultivation proceeds in equal proportion to what it has done since Chilicothe was first laid out, about ten years ago, must in a short time present one of the finest landscapes imaginable."

From Chilicothe, on the State road, to Point Falls, is eighteen miles. At these falls is the town of Bainbridge, consisting of about twenty houses, where there is a post-office. The falls will admit of extensive water-works, and the country around them consists of a rich soil. Two miles below the falls, Point river has washed away the side of a hill that bordered on the bank, which has exposed to view a great variety of fossils. The hill, which is supposed to be nearly 400 feet high, seems to consist principally of lamina of slate stone. These lamina appear to be cemented together by allum and copperas, which is melted and runs out by the heat of the sun. It is collected by the inhabitants and applied to common use. There are round lumps of a mineral substance, from the size of a turkey's egg to that of a large common ball, frequently rolling down, which appear to contain sulphur, lead, and copper. In the vicinity of Point river, which runs into the Scioto, are a great variety of ochres and pigments of different colours, as well as minerals, which would afford an ample field for the investigation of the mineralogists. Many sulphur springs gush out from the hills in the neighbourhood of this river.

South of the State road, and between Point and the Ohio, is a large range of steep hills, called the Sunfish Hills, from a stream of that name which drains them and discharges itself into the Ohio. They are about forty miles wide from Point to the Ohio, and about sixty miles long from the Scioto to the Little Miami. The greater part of these hills are so steep and broken that no settlements can be made upon them. But in those parts of them which will admit of cultivation, the land is rich, clothed with excellent timber, and the settlements rapidly increasing.

From the falls of Point to West Union, the land is hilly, but the soil good and thickly settled. The town is situated on the declivity of a hill, consisting of about sixty houses, mostly of hewed logs, a log court house and jail, and is the seat of justice of the county of Adams. From West Union to the Ohio, opposite Limestone, in Kentucky, on the great road, the land is mostly hilly, the soil rich and clothed with large timber, principally oak and hickory.

The lands north of Chilicothe and the State road to Limestone, are, for about twenty miles, moderately hilly, soil good, producing all the variety of timber common to the State, excepting pine. North of this tract commences the large prairie, or natural meadow ; which extends from the Scioto to the Little Miami, a distance of sixty miles, and nearly an hundred miles in a northern direction. This meadow has a level appearance, but is somewhat an inclined plain, which produces a more rapid current in the streams of water than would be expected. Several branches of the Miami and Scioto take their rise in this plain, which is not sunk into swampy land, but most of it sufficiently dry for culture. It is covered with long coarse grass. Cattle feed eagerly on it, and fatten as well as in good pastures. Large droves are brought every spring from Kentucky, and fattened here for the fall market. The soil produces good corn, and if properly cultivated woul probably produce large crops of hemp. Som parts are sprinkled over with a light growth c small oaks and hickory. In other parts it is s entirely destitute of any growth of wood, that for a great distance not a single tree is to be seen It so much resembles an old settled country, tha the traveller is constantly looking out for fence and buildings.

The town of Franklinton is situated at the fork of the Scioto, forty-five miles above Chilicothe by land, and about seventy by water. It was laid out about the year 1798, by Lucas Sullivan, Esq on the west bank of the Scioto, opposite to the mouth of Whetstone river, and on a beautiful swell of ground, which gradually depends in every direction from the centre of the town. It contains about an hundred houses, ten or twelve of which are built of brick. It is the seat of justice for the county of Franklin, and has a handsome brick court house, with a neat cupola. On one side of the town is a delightful prairie, and on the other the river Scioto, which renders the prospect highly pleasing. The land around Franklinton, in every direction, is rich and level, but, at a few miles distant, wood and timber become scarce.

Worthington is nine miles distant on the Whetstone river. It was laid out about the year 1805, by the Rev. James Kilboun and others from Connecticut. The land in the vicinity of this town is very rich and level, covered with a large growth of timber, principally beach, sugar maple, and ash. It produces excellent corn, rye, wheat, hemp, flax, and all kinds of vegetables, and will probably be highly favourable to fruit trees. This town has settled with unusual rapidity.

About sixteen miles northeast of Worthington, is the town of Bixby, a new, but very growing settlement. It has much the same face of country and soil with that of Worthington.

Upon the main branch of the Scioto, thirty-six miles from Franklinton, and near the Indian boundary line, is the town of Delaware, the seat of justice for the county of that name. It is situated on the east bank of the river, and the land level and good in every direction near it, but at present thinly settled.

The Scioto has no falls from the mouth to its source, and glides with a gentle current, the greater part of the distance, over a sandy bottom. It abounds with fish, mostly of the perch and sucker kind, but cat-fish and pike are frequently caught. Near Chilicothe, eighty barrels of the fish called white perch were taken out of one deep place in a day.

The next considerable river, westward, which runs from the northward into the Ohio, is the Little Miami. Its banks are high, and has good land on its borders, but has not a sufficient depth of water for batteaux or boats.

The county of Highland lies on the east side of this river and south of the great prairie, extending eastward within twenty miles of Chilicothe. It is moderately hilly, the soil rich, and the growth of timber generally large. Hillsborough is the seat of justice, and contains about thirty houses, and a handsome brick court house. A tract of swaly, wet land, about eight miles in width, passes through the country, which drains a part of the great prairie. Its waters run off by Oak creek into the Ohio. The road from Chilicothe to Cincinnati passes through it, and the depth of mud and water renders travelling extremely troublesome at all seasons of the year.

The people settled between the Scioto and Little Miami are mostly from Virginia and Kentucky, and the improvements are inconsiderable, excepting near Chilicothe.

Immediately below the mouth of the Little Miami, is the town of Columbia. It was laid out by Col. Symmes, and is the oldest settlement in the State, on the Ohio river, except Marietta; but has increased very little in the number of its inhabitants.

At present, it is only a neat, pleasant village, consisting of about forty houses, built at some distance from each other, on a rich bottom or interval. Nor is it probable, from its situation, that it will ever become a place of much business.

On an eastern branch of the Little Miami, is Williamsburge, the seat of justice for Clermont county, containing about fifty houses, and a handsome stone court house. The face of the country is hilly, but the soil is rich, especially on the banks of the river, where the lands are very fine.

Further up the Miami is Lebanon, situated on the bank, and the largest town on this river. It contains about an hundred houses and is inhabited by the people called Shaking Quakers. They are emigrants from Kentucky, who were first formed into a regular society by a Mr. Macnamara, who still continues to be their head. They have acquired much credit, as a frugal, industrious people.

About twenty-five miles above Lebanon, is Zenia, situated on the bank of the Miami, and is the seat of justice for the county of Greene. It contains about fifty houses and a handsome court house. The country around it is level and fertile. Nine miles above this town is a very singular spring. It issues near the brow of an high, flat topped hill, about a mile from the western bank of the river. Water sufficient to carry an over-shot mill issues from it, and the quantity has never been known to increase or diminish. It throws out a reddish sediment, which concretes into a hard mass, forming a kind of bank, which frequently alters the position of the spring. The side of the hill is very steep, and the elevation of the spring from the base of the hill is about eighty feet. The water is very cold and has a strange taste of iron and copper. It is in high repute for its medicinal virtues, and is become a place of considerable resort.

The land further up the river is level and the growth principally oak. Although the soil is rather thin, it produces good wheat. Springfield is about twenty miles above Zenia, consisting of about fifty houses and the most of them well built. It is situated on the forks of Mad river. From Sringfield to Urbana is fourteen miles. The land north of Springfield is much richer than that which lies south of it. Here the growth varies from oak to beach, ash, sugar-maple, black and white walnut, and cherry. Urbana is the seat of justice for the county of Champaign. It contains about sixty houses and is rapidly increasing in inhabitants. From this town to the Indian boundary line is about sixty miles; the land mostly level, the growth large, inclining to beach, the water good, and will admit of many excellent mill seats.

Returning back to the Ohio, the first town below Columbia is Cincinnati, five miles distant. In the Ohio Navigator a concise and correct description is given of this town.

"Cincinnati is handsomely situated on a first and second bank of the Ohio, opposite Licking river. It is a flourishing town, has a rich, level, and well settled country around it. It contains about four hundred dwellings, an elegant court house, jail, three market houses, a land office for the sale of Congress lands, two printing offices, issuing weekly Gazettes, thirty mercantile stores, and the various branches of mechanism are carried on with spirit. Industry of every kind being duly encouraged by the citizens, Cincinnati is likely to become a considerable manufacturing place. It is eighty-two miles north by east from Frankfort, and about three hundred and eighty by land south southwest from Pittsburgh, north latitude thirty-nine degrees, five minutes, fifty-four seconds, according to Mr. Ellicot, and west longitude eighty-five degrees, forty-four minutes. It is the principal town in what is called Symmes's purchase, and is the seat of justice for what is called Hamilton county, Ohio. It has a bank issuing notes under the authority of the State, called *The Miami Exporting company*. The healthiness and salubrity of the climate; the levelness and luxuriance of the soil; the purity and excellence of the waters, added to the blessings attendant on the judicious administration of mild and equitable laws; the great security in the land titles; all seem to centre in a favourable point of expectation, that Cincinnati and the country around it, must one day become rich and very populous, equal perhaps, if not superior to any other place of an interior in the United States. The site of Fort Washington is near the centre of the town. It was a principal frontier post; it is now laid out in town lots." A considerable trade is carried on between Cincinnati and New

Orleans in keel boats, which return laden with foreign goods. The passage of a boat of forty tons down to New Orleans is computed at about twenty-five, and its return to Cincinnati at about sixty-five days.

From Cincinnati to North Bend, on the Ohio, is sixteen miles; and to the mouth of the Great Miami, where the west boundary line of the State meets the Ohio, is seven miles further. This tract of land, which extends some distance from the Ohio, is interval of the first quality; well settled, and in a high state of cultivation. Receding farther back from the Ohio, the land is hilly, the soil indifferent, and thinly settled. The road up the Great Miami leaves the Ohio at Cincinnati, and comes to the Miami at Hamilton, fourteen miles distant. Hamilton is the spot where fort Hamilton formerly stood. It is situated on a large plain, well cultivated, but does not contain more than ten or fifteen houses. It has been a considerable village, but since Cincinnati has so rapidly increased, Hamilton has been on the decline. Thirty-five miles above Hamilton is Franklin, on the Great Miami, containing about sixty houses, built on one street. The lands in its vicinity are level and rich, and have some of the best cultivated farms in the State. Dayton is thirty miles above Franklin; the country more level than below, and the lands well settled and improved. The town is situated on the east branch of the Great Miami at the mouth of Mad river. Its situation is pleasant, being surrounded by a rich country, and bids fair to become a place of considerable business. It contains about eighty houses, the most of which are neatly built. It is the seat of justice for the county of Montgomery. On the west side of the Miami, a little above Dayton, comes in a large branch, called Stillwater. This branch extends from the Miami, in a westerly direction, beyond the line of the State, which is about forty miles distant. Within the State, the lands on this branch are rich and level. This tract has been settled by a number of French or Quakers, who emigrated from the States of South Carolina or Georgia. In the habits of industry and œconomy, they devoted themselves to the cultivation of the land, and have made great improvements. The tract is thickly settled and very productive. So large a settlement by these quiet, peaceable inhabitants has been a valuable acquisition of the State.

From Dayton to the Indian line, north, is about fifty miles. The lands are mostly level and rich. From the Indian boundary the lands are generally level to the head waters of the stream which run into lake Erie. Some portion of this tract of country is inundated in the winter and spring for two or three months. The head waters of the main branch of the Great Miami, called Leromie's creek communicate, by a short portage, with Au Glaize, which runs into the Miami of the lakes, and another branch, by a portage of somewhat greater length, with Sandusky river. The portage is likewise short from the Scioto to this river, and great advantages are expected to result to the State of Ohio, in future time, by a communication between the waters which descend to the Ohio, and those which run into the lakes.

The waters of the Great Miami are not interrupted by falls, or considerable rapids for three hundred miles. Large boats can pass from Dayton to the Ohio, the greater part of the year. But being subject to a much greater decrease of water, it is less favourable to navigation than the Muskingum, nor is the river equally good for the passage of boats at any season. This river furnishes excellent fish, mostly of the same kind, but somewhat of a greater variety, than the Scioto. Considerable quantities of fine fish are taken in the Little Miami, which afford a good supply for the market, at Cincinnati, in summer and autumn.

The streams in every part of the State are well stocked with fish of various kinds. The most of them appear, at least, specifically different from those in the waters of the Atlantic States. But similar names are applied to many of them. The black and yellow cat-fish are of the largest size, and weigh from four or five to more than one hundred pounds. They nearly resemble the pout of New England. The pike differ little from those over the mountains in form, but are much larger. Some have been caught of thirty or forty pounds weight. There are fish called perch, sturgeon, bass, and salmon, but differ from those fish in the northern States. The buffaloe fish seem to be peculiar to these waters, and are said to be so called on account of a noise they make in the water, resembling a buffaloe.

The State undoubtedly abounds in a great variety of fossils, such as clayes, ochres, pigments, and the most useful ores, but it has been very little explored. The waters of the Scioto, and some parts of the Ohio, particularly the rapids, possess a petrifying quality. Pieces of wood, small fish, and other animals, have been found completely changed into stone. The bones of animals of an enormous size, and some of the skeletons nearly complete, have been dug up in several places, particularly at Big Bone creek, on the left bank of the Ohio.

The quadrupeds which are native are the buffaloe, elk, red deer,* bear, wolf, grey and black fox, panther, wild cat, rackoon, beaver, porcupine, ground hog, grey and black squirrels, and those smaller animals which are found in similar climates. As the settlements have advanced, the buffaloe and elk have retreated into the uncultivated country. Grey and black squirrels still continue in prodigious numbers. They

*The fawns, when very young, are often found asleep alone in the woods. If caught while napping and carried some distance, they may be put down, and will follow the hunter as readily as his dog, and come and eat bread out of his hand. In this way the deer are easily domesticated.

are frequently seen swimming across the largest rivers, and are extremely destructive to fields of Indian corn.

Of the winged fowls, the swan and pelican are sometimes seen; geese, brant, and ducks of various species, are found in the rivers; turkies, pheasants, partridges, and quails in abundance, in the forests. Turkies are still in great plenty, though perhaps not so numerous, as before the settlements commenced. They are of a large size, and the flesh of an excellent flavour. Large flocks visit the wheat fields after sowing, and at the time of harvest, and often greatly injure the crop. When their eggs are hatched under hens, the turkey chickens will be tame, and in this way the wild turkey is easily domesticated. The pigeons are so numerous as almost to exceed credibility. At certain times in the year, vast flights resort to particular places, called pigeon roosts. Many of these roosts extend over more than an hundred acres of land, and it is said, some have been found to exceed a thousand acres. They light upon the trees in such numbers as to fill all the branches, and, by their weight, break off large limbs. Every tree in these extended roosts is killed, and the dung on the ground, which has been found from twelve to eighteen inches deep, destroying every species of vegetation beneath them. The green paroquet with a yellow crown, a species of the parrot, is very common. It has a harsh, unpleasant note, and although easily tamed, it cannot be taught to imitate the human voice. The habits of these birds are in some respect singular. They are always seen in flocks, which retire, at night, into hollow trees, frequently in large numbers, where they suspend themselves by their bills. These flocks also retreat to hollow trees in the winter. There have been found after a severe winter, prodigious numbers in a large tree, filling the whole cavity, where they had perished by the severity of the cold.* There are a great variety of other large and small birds, but the most of them are similar to those which are indigenous in the northern and middle Atlantic States.

Some of the people, who first emigrated into this country, had fearful apprehensions of venomous serpents, but were soon relieved on their arrival. The snakes are very nearly of the same kind, which are found in the middle and northern Atlantic States; probably not so numerous as they were there, on their first settlement. The black and yellow rattle snakes are found in the Ohio State, but are not very often seen, except it be near the places where they have dens. The copper-heads are more frequently met with, about the trunks of fallen trees and about rubbish, under which they retreat in the winter. They resemble the rattle snake in colour, but not so large, are

* The large collection of feathers found in a hollow tree, in Waterford, and examined by the Rev. Mr. Harris, were probably the feathers of these birds. *Harris' Journal of a Tour to the Ohio* Page 100.

less active and destitute of rattles. Their bite is not considered so dangerous as that of the rattle snake. They have five or six very small poisonous teeth, placed in the same sack, on each side of the upper jaw; the rattle snake has only one on each side, but are very large. The moccason snake, which is very common in the Carolinas, has been seen in some parts of the State, but very rarely. In the prairies, a very small rattle snake, about the size of a man's finger, and ten or twelve inches in length, is frequently found among the grass. They are called the prairie rattle snake, and are said to be venomous. These are all the poisonous snakes found in this country. There are two kinds of water snake; the backs are black, and the belly of the one is a bright red, and of the other of an ash colour. The other snakes are the common black snakes; some with a ring round the neck, but the most of them have none; the striped and green snake, and the speckled snake, usually called the house adder. Lizards, of various colours, and some of them very beautiful and active, are plenty. At the falls of Point Creek, a remarkably large water lizard has been taken with the hook, while fishing for the cat and other fish. The form is that of a lizard; the skin, in colour and smoothness, resembles the New England pout; the legs short, and the tail flattened like an eel. When a pressure is made on the body, thick, milky matter, in large drops, and perfectly white, exudes from the pores of the skin. Some have been caught of eight or ten pounds weight. They are not amphibious, for they will not live longer out of the water than the pout or eel. The other reptiles, and the great variety of insects, found in this country, do not appear materially to differ from those of the Atlantic States.

A

TOPOGRAPHICAL DESCRIPTION

OF THE

INDIANA TERRITORY.

This part of the northwestern country was constituted a territorial government, by an act of Congress, passed the 7th day of May, 1800, and was bounded eastwardly by the following line of separation; viz. "All that part of the territory of the United States, northwest of the Ohio river which lies westward of a line beginning at the Ohio, opposite to the mouth of the Kentucky river, and running thence to fort Recovery, and thence north until it shall intersect the territorial line between the United States and Canada, shall, for the purpose of a temporary government, constitute a separate territory, and be called the Indiana Territory. And Saint Vincennes, on the Wabash river, shall be the seat of the government." Only the eastern boundary is named in the act, and the Indian claim of a large portion of the Territory is not extinguished. The whole tract, agreeable to this line, is bounded south by the Ohio, west by the Mississippi, and north by the line between the United States and Canada, which makes the extent of this Territory considerably greater than the State of Ohio.

The general face of the country approaches to a level, but some parts of it are hilly. It has a number of large, navigable rivers meandering through it to the Ohio and Mississippi, and many smaller streams, some of which run into the lakes.

The Wabash is a large river, rising near the head waters of the river St. Joseph, and the Miami at the lakes, and running in a southwesterly direction empties into the Ohio, about four hundred and seventy miles below the Great Miami river. It is four hundred yards wide at the mouth, and navigable for keel boats, about four hundred miles, to Ouiatan, an ancient French village; and from this village, with small craft, to a portage on a south branch, which forms a communication with the Miami that runs into Lake Erie. This portage is eight miles, and comes to the Miami near Fort Wayne.

From a north branch, by a short portage, a communication is made with the river Saint Joseph, running into Lake Michigan. The Wabash is replenished with numerous tributary streams, and has generally, a gentle current above Saint Vincennes. Below are several rapids. Those which principally obstruct the navigation are between Saint Vincennes and White river, called the great Rapids. Near the village Ouiatan, it is said a silver mine has been discovered, which it is apprehended will prove valuable. About forty miles below the village comes in the river Vermillion Jaune. On this river is the residence of the much famed Indian Prophet. The town in which he lives is large for an Indian village, and has received the name of the *Prophet's town.* Much of the land on the Wabash is rich and well timbered, but towards the head waters there is less timber, and very fertile and extensive prairies. A white and blue clay of an excellent quality is said to abound on this river. There are many salt springs, and plenty of lime and free stone.

Saint Vincennes is a handsome town, about an hundred miles from the mouth of the river, situated on the east bank, upon a beautiful, level, and rich spot of ground. It is the largest town in the Territory, and is made the seat of government. This was an ancient French fortress, called Post Saint Vincennes. Since the American revolution the town has been repaired and enlarged, and is now a very thriving place, but the inhabitants still are mostly French. There are more than an hundred houses, some of which are built of free stone, in a handsome style, a considerable number of merchantile stores, a post office and printing office. Here, a profitable trade is carried on in furs and peltry. The situation is healthy, the winters mild, and the rich and highly cultivated lands around it are delightful.

About forty miles from Saint Vincennes, in a southwesterly direction, is the Great Sabine, so called, where salt, in large quantities, is made. It is situated in hilly land, on a stream of water which flows into the Ohio. The land is still owned by the government of the United States, but rented to those who carry on the salt works, and who are said to obligate themselves to make, at least, a certain quantity annually, and are not permitted to sell it for more than at a stipulated price. The waters in this Saline are said to have double the strength of those at the great salt springs on the Scioto river.

The land on the Indiana side, bordering on the Ohio river, from the Great Miami nearly to the Mississippi, a distance of about six hundred miles, is generally hilly and broken, but some excellent bottoms, of different extent, are interspersed. From a small distance above fort Massai and down to the mouth of the Ohio, the land gradually becomes level, forming a rich and delightful prairie. In this distance, there are many small streams, but no considerable river, excepting the Wabash, which falls into the Ohio.

But on the opposite side, within a less distance three large, navigable rivers, besides numerous smaller streams, contribute their waters to the Ohio. The first is Kentucky river, which comes in about seventy miles following the bends of the river below the Great Miami, is ninety yards wide at its mouth, and the same width, when the water is high, eighty miles above. It is navigable for loaded boats, at a high stage of the water, two hundred miles. The second is the Cumberland, or Shawnee river, which falls into the Ohio about five hundred miles below the Kentucky river, and four hundred miles below the Rapids, and is three hundred yards wide at its mouth. There being no obstructions, and having a fine gentle current, ships of four hundred tons can descend in times of floods from the distance of about four hundred miles into the Ohio. The third is the Tennessee, or Cherokee river, which enters the Ohio, about twelve miles below the Cumberland; and is five hundred yards wide at its mouth. This is the largest river that empties into the Ohio. It is computed to be navigable for boats one thousand miles, and will admit vessels of considerable burden as far as the Muscle Shoals, which is two hundred and fifty miles from its mouth.

On the Indiana side of the Ohio, there are only some scattering settlements, excepting Jeffersonville, and Clarksville, two small villages, at the Rapids, one hundred and fifty miles below the Great Miami. Jeffersonville is situated in the bend of the river, on an high bank, just above the Rapids, where pilots are taken off for conducting vessels over them. It is a post town, but contains only a small number of inhabitants, and probably will never be a thriving place. Clarksville is another small village immediately below the Rapids, and opposite the elbow at Shippingport. In time it may become a place of considerable business. On the opposite bank, about midway between these two villages and opposite the Rapids, is Louisville, which is much larger, and bids fair to become a flourishing town. It is situated on an elevated plain, and contains about one hundred and fifty houses, a printing and a post office. It is a port of entry, and has a considerable number of mercantile stores, and several ware houses for storing goods. Shippingport is on the same side, at the foot of the falls. Here, boats generally make a landing after passing the Rapids. Ship building was began and was carried on with considerable spirit here, until it received a check by the late embargo law. Having an excellent harbour, the situation appears eligible for prosecuting this business to advantage.

The Rapids are occasioned by a ledge of rocks extending entirely across the river, and is the most dangerous place for navigation, in the whole extent of the Ohio river. The distance over them is about two miles, and the descent from a level above is twenty-two feet and a half. When the water is high the fall is only perceived by an increased velocity of the vessel, which is computed to be at the rate of about ten or twelve miles an hour. When the water is low, a large portion of the rocks are seen, and it is then that the passage becomes dangerous. There are three channels.

One is on the north side, called Indian *Schute*, and is the main channel, but not passable when the water is high; another is near the middle of the river, and called the Middle *Schute*, and is safe and easy in all heights of water above the middle stage. The third is on the south side, called the Kentucky *Schute*, and is only passable when the water is high. Immediately above the falls, in the mouth of Beargrass creek, is a good harbour, having twelve feet of water in the lowest stage of the river. At the foot of the falls is another harbour, called Rock Harbour, with water sufficient, at all times, for vessels of any burden. These two harbours are of the greatest importance to those who have occasion to navigate this dangerous passage.

Opening a channel for the passage of ships by the Rapids has been seriously contemplated; which would be of immense advantage to the trade of the Ohio. That it is practicable cannot be doubted. The only difficulty seems to be to raise a fund sufficient for the purpose. It has been principally proposed to open the canal on the Kentucky side, to commence below Beargrass creek, and enter the river below Shippingport, a distance of about one mile and three quarters; and that it should be sufficient for ships of four hundred tons. The ground through which it would pass is a stiff clay, down to within about three feet of the flower of the canals which then is a rock. The average depth of the canal is computed at about twenty-one feet, in order to admit a column of water three feet by twenty-four, at the lowest stage of the river.*

In passing down the Ohio, about forty miles below the Wabash, a curious cave is seen in a high bank, on the Indiana side. Its mouth opens to the river, and when the water is high it nearly flows into it. The entrance is an arch in a rock about twenty-five feet high in the centre, eighty feet wide at the base, and extending back from the opening one hundred and eighty feet. The mouth is darkened by several large trees growing before it, which give it a gloomy and solemn appearance. Passengers usually visit it, and have engraved on the sides within the mouth, a great number of names, dates and other inscriptions. Indian superstition and other fabulous stories reported respecting this cave do not merit a repetition.

Further down the river, and within forty-six miles of its mouth, is fort Massac, situated on a high commanding bank, where a Lieutenant's command is stationed. It was originally built by the French. Here the land is rich and level, consisting principally of natural meadow, with

* In the Ohio Navigator a very accurate description is given of the Rapids with an excellent map of the falls. From this description the account of them here given, is principally taken. To this very valuable work, the writer is indebted for many observations respecting the Ohio and Mississippi rivers, and for much information in regard to the country bordering upon them.

some beautiful groves, or copses of large trees. Near the fort, and along the banks of the river there are a number of settlers, who have well cultivated gardens and fields, which are very productive. At a small distance below, is Wilkersonville, situated on a bluff, formerly called Cedar Bluffs, but has very few inhabitants.

On the river Mississippi, the first settlement of any note in the Indiana Territory, is the village Kaskaskia. It is an ancient French town, about ninety miles above the mouth of the Ohio, situated on the Kaskaskia river, at the distance of five miles from the Mississippi. The village contains about one hundred houses, and the inhabitants principally French. In the vicinity of this village the land is excellent and highly cultivated. The river Kaskaskia is navigable about one hundred miles, and drains an extensive tract of level country. There is a road leading from Saint Vincennes to the Kaskaskia village, nearly in a west direction. This road passes through almost one continued prairie for about two hundred miles, there being only scattered copses of wood, which have the appearance of small islands, in a wide extended bay. These natural meadows are covered with a tall grass, and the sun appears to rise and set in the grass. On this road there are few settlers, and the traveller is obliged, for several nights, to lodge in the grass or copses of wood. In this prairie, large herds of buffaloe, elk, and deer, may be seen grazing nearly the whole of the year.

Cahokia is another small village, sixty miles further up the Mississippi, and inhabited by French people. It is situated on a small stream, about a mile from the river, and contains about eighty houses. The land here is rich, mostly level, and covered with large timber.

The Illinois, a noble river, enters the Mississippi forty-five miles further up, and twenty-five miles above the mouth of the Missouri. It is four hundred yards wide at its mouth, and is navigable four hundred and fifty miles. Numerous tributary streams fall into it on both sides, some of which are also navigable a considerable distance. The Little Michilimackinac enters the river, from the southward, one hundred and ninety miles from the mouth, and is navigable ninety miles. One of the principal branches of the Illinois takes its rise near the head waters of the Chichago river, which enters into lake Michigan. Between these two rivers, there is a short portage of only two miles, making an easy communication between the Mississippi and the lakes. The navigation is uninterrupted, for vessels of considerable burden, from Lake Michigan to Niagara falls. From Lake Erie, to the Mohawk river, which empties into the Hudson, it is said, all the portages do not exceed twenty-six miles. Thus, by portages of about twenty-eight miles, an inland navigation is opened between New Orleans and

New York; a distance computed to be nearly four thousand miles. Perhaps there is not to be found an inland navigation of equal extent, in any part of the world. Another large branch of the Illinois rises near the river Saint Joseph, passing south of Lake Michigan, where a portage may be easily formed. It is called the Theakiki river.

The banks of the Illinois are generally high. The bed of the river being a white marble, or clay, or sand, the waters are remarkably clear. It abounds with beautiful islands, one of which is ten miles long; and adjoining or near to it, are many coal mines, salt ponds, and small lakes. It passes through one lake, two hundred and ten miles from its mouth, which is twenty miles in length, and three or four miles in breadth, called Illinois lake. The river, and waters communicating with it, are replenished with a variety of excellent fish. The large tract of country through which this river and its branches meander, is said not to be exceeded in beauty, levelness, richness, and fertility of soil, by any tract of land, of equal extent, in the United States. From the Illinois to the Wabash, excepting some little distance from the rivers, is almost one continued prairie, or natural meadow, intermixed with groves, or copses of wood, and some swamps and small lakes. These beautiful, and, to the eye of the beholder, unlimited fields, are covered with a luxuriant growth of grass, and other vegetable productions, which afford fattening and plentiful grazing for innumerable herds of buffaloe, elk, and deer. All the variety of forest trees and shrubs, common to the western country, are found in some parts of the Indiana Territory; but different kinds abound more in some situations and soils than in others. There is also a great difference in the size of the growth of the same kind of trees, in different soils. In the neighbourhood of the Illinois the crab-apple, plumb, and cherry trees grow in great plenty, yielding fruit in abundance. Here the grape vine flourishes admirably, producing large quantities of grapes, of which the inhabitants make a good red wine, for their own consumption. It is said in the year 1769, one hundred and ten hogsheads of well tasted and strong wine were made by the French settlers, from the grapes. The sugar-maple, and black and white mulberry grow in plenty.

The settlers on this river are almost entirely French people, who live principally in small villages. Where the land is cultivated, it yields large crops of almost every article they commit to the ground. It has been found that tobacco, indigo, hemp, and flax, can be raised here to much advantage.

Between the Illinois and the falls of Saint Anthony, a distance of about eight hundred and seventy miles, there are a large number of considerable streams, and some of them navigable rivers, which come from the eastward and discharge their waters into the Mississippi. The following are the largest navigable rivers, and the computed distance from each other, with the distance they are said to be navigable. The first is Rocky river, or Riviere a la Roche, one hundred and sixty miles above the Illinois. This is a large river, but the navigation is said to be impeded by rocks and rapids. The second is Mine river, or Riviere, a la Mine, two hundred and ten miles above Rocky river, and navigable fifty miles. The third is Ouiconsin, one hundred and twenty miles further up, navigable two hundred miles. A bend in this river, near its head waters, passes so near to a bend in Fose river, which empties into Green Bay, a branch of Lake Michigan, that the portage is said to be only one mile and three quarters, forming another easy communication between the Mississippi and the lakes. The fourth, Black river, one hundred and fifty miles further, and navigable one hundred miles. The fifth, is the river Chippeway, sixty-five miles above Black river, and navigable one hundred miles. The sixth, is Sotoux river, only fifteen miles further up, and navigable eighty miles. The mouth of this river is said to be three hundred and eighty yards wide. The seventh, is the Saint Croix, further distant sixty miles, and is said to be navigable one hundred miles. The mouth of this river is two hundred yards. From the Saint Croix to Saint Anthony's falls, is ninety miles, which is in forty-five degrees of north latitude.

North of the Illinois the country gradually becomes hilly, and near to Lake Superior, are mountains of very considerable attitude. It is inhabited by numerous bands of Indians, of different nations; some wandering bands, others live in villages conveniently situated for hunting excursions. It has been said that near some of these large rivers, lead ore has been found in large quantities, and that in some places copper ore has been discovered of a very great degree of purity. But this extensive tract of country has been very little explored. Almost the only white people who have visited it, have been the traders in furs and peltry.

A

DESCRIPTION

OF THE

MISSISSIPPI RIVER.

This noble river was made the western boundary of the United States, by the definitive treaty with Great Britain, in the year 1783. Considering its great length, the prodigious column of water rolling in its deep channel, and the quantity discharged by numerous outlets, it must be rated among the largest rivers on the American continent. It has been called the American Nile, from some resemblance it seems to bear to that celebrated river in Egypt. The fertility of Egypt is well known to be owing to the periodical overflowing of the Nile. From a similar course, vast tracts of land have been enriched by the outlets and overflowing of the Mississippi. The Nile begins to rise about the middle of June, and to subside in September. The floods in the Mississippi begin about the first of April, and the water falls within its banks by the first of August. The overflowing is much greater on the western, than on the eastern side of the river. From New Madrid to Pointe Coupee, a distance of more than eight hundred miles, the land on the western bank, with the exception of a few small tracts, is overflowed in the spring. In some parts the inundation extends fifty miles back from the river, covering vast cypress swamps, and lands producing different kinds of wood, with a depth of from two to twelve feet of water. No considerable settlements for this distance can be formed on the bank of the river. But much of the bank on the eastern side rises above the highest floods, and will admit of settlements and improvement. The waters of the Nile are extolled by the Egyptians, on account of their wholesome qualities and pleasant taste. The waters of the Mississippi, after filtration, or being in any way purified from a muddy sediment, are not disagreeable to the taste, especially to those who have been habituated to them. They are supposed to be possessed of medical properties, operating on some people as a mild cathartic, and generally cleansing the skin from curtaneous eruptions.

It is supposed the Mississippi takes its rise in a lake called White Bear Lake, but its head waters appear not to have been very accurately explored. The most that is known is derived from Indian information. The river above the falls of Saint Anthony, is called, by the Indians, Blue river. Here the stream is remarkably clear, and said to be navigable above the falls for three hundred miles. These falls were first visited by Father Louis Hennipin, a French Missionary, about the year 1680, who was the first European ever seen by the natives, and who gave them the name of Saint Anthony's falls. The country adjacent approaches to a plain, with some swelling hills. At the falls the river is two hundred and fifty yards wide, and the perpendicular descent of the water about thirty feet. Near the falls the prospect is said to be highly picturesque and delightful. This widely expanded sheet of water may be seen several miles below, where the eye of the beholder is struck with pleasing admiration, and views, with rapture, this romantic scene. At these falls a large factory is established, where many of the western bands of Indians bring their furs and peltry, to exchange for various kinds of merchandise.

About ten miles below the falls enters the large river Saint Peters, from the westward. The mouth of this river is one hundred yards wide, and the current deep. It is said that it holds its depth and width very nearly for two hundred miles. Further up, several branches come in; the head waters of some of which are said to take their rise near the streams which run into the Missouri. On this river and its branches are several trading posts, where Indians who reside on the Missouri frequently resort for commerce.

At a small distance above the mouth of the river Chippeway, is a lake, about twenty miles in length and six miles in breadth, called lake Pepin. The Mississippi passes through this lake, and although the French have denominated it a lake, it has rather the appearance of an extended width of the river. The water in some parts of it is deep, and abounds with several kinds of excellent fish. Large numbers of fowl, such as storks, swan, geese, ducks, and brant, resort to this lake. The groves and plains around it are replenished with turkies and partridges.

Below the lake, the river glides with a gentle current, having alternately high lands on one side, and extended meadows on the other. Some of the precipices fronting the river, are high and steep, ascending like pyramids, and exhibiting the appearance of ancient towers. Descending down the river, the eye is delighted, in some places, with the view of large, rich prairies, extending far back towards distant mountains, with beautiful groves or copses of trees, scattered over them, and watered with a number of small lakes.

Between the Saint Peters and Missouri rivers, many streams of considerable magnitude enter the Mississippi from the westward. The largest of them is the river Moin, about one hundred miles above the mouth of the Illinois. On this river the Sioux, and some other bands of Indians, frequently descend with their furs and skins for market. The current of the Mississippi continues gentle, and its water clear, until it joins the Missouri, where it becomes much more rapid, and remarkably cold and muddy. At the common stage of the waters, in these two streams, the Missouri is supposed to be the largest river. This junction is formed twenty-five miles below the Illinois, and two hundred and thirty miles above the Ohio.

The land on the banks of the Missouri are rich, and where they are well cultivated, exceedingly productive. There are two settlements, Saint Charles and Saint Andrew, principally inhabited by emigrants from Kentucky. Other small settlements have commenced further up the river. The most distant settlement of white people is Saint John's, which is one hundred miles from its mouth. The great extent of this river was unknown until it was explored by Captain Lewis, and Captain Clark. Traders had before ascended two thousand miles, but Captain Lewis computes the distance from the mouth to the great falls, to be two thousand five hundred and seventy-five miles. About one hundred miles above Saint John's, the river becomes broad, being eight hundred and seventy-five yards wide, where the Osage river enters; but about fifty miles further up it narrows again to about three hundred yards. The Osage comes in from the south, and is one hundred and ninety-seven yards wide at its mouth. The Osage Indians reside on this river, from whom it takes its name, about two hundred miles from its mouth. Here the extensive prairies commence, wholly destitute of trees, but covered with tall grass, and continue, with little interruption, far towards the borders of New Mexico, and the Rocky Mountains.

Fifteen miles below the mouth of the Missouri, is Saint Louis, delightfully situated on elevated ground, upon the bank of the Mississippi. It is considered to be the most healthy and pleasant situation known in this part of the country. The settlement of this village was began by a few French people, who came over from the east side of the river, about the year 1765. It became the residence of the Spanish Commandant, and of the principal Indian traders. The trade of the Indians on the Missouri, part of the Mississippi, and Illinois, was chiefly drawn to this village. Before the purchase of Louisiana by the United States, it contained one hundred and twenty houses, mostly built of stone, but large and commodious dwellings. It contained about eight hundred inhabitants, who were mostly French. Since this purchase was made, numbers have emigrated to this village from different parts of the United States. There are now more than two hundred houses, a post office, and a printing office, issuing a Weekly Gazette. There are many mercantile stores, and a flourishing trade in furs and peltry. It is made the seat of territorial government for Upper Louisiana.

Saint Genevieve, or Missire is sixty-four miles lower down, on the bank of the Mississippi, and nearly opposite the village of Kaskaskia. It is a considerable village, containing more than two hundred houses. In the year 1773, this and Saint Louis were the only villages on the western side of the river. At a short distance below is a small settlement, called the Saline, where large quantities of salt are made, and sold at the works for about one dollar per bushel. Not far from Saint Genevieve, in a western direction, a large number of lead furnaces are worked, producing great quantities of lead, where it may be purchased at three or four cents per pound. In various parts of a large tract of country south of the Missouri, numerous lead mines are to be found. Many of them are not more than two or three feet below the surface, and may be worked with great ease. Were the inhabitants sufficiently numerous to work the mines, it is supposed a quantity of lead might be obtained from the ore, equal to the supply of all Europe.

The principal mines which have yet been worked, are near the head waters and branches of the river Marameg. This river is of considerable size; it enters the Mississippi about twenty miles below Saint Louis; it comes in nearly in the direction of the Missouri; and its widely extended branches reach far back into the country. About forty miles from Saint Genevieve, on a branch of the Marameg, is Barton's mine, discovered by Francis Barton, who obtained a grant of the land, and began to work the ore nearly forty years ago. It is now in the possession of a Mr.

Austin, who has erected a good smelting furnace. This ore is not of the richest kind, but a greater quantity has been worked here, than in any other part of the country, from which the owner has derived great profits. The ore is taken out of the ground in an open prairie which is elevated nearly one hundred feet above the bed of the creek, and is supposed to extend over some thousands of acres. The mineral is found within two feet of the surface, in a strata of gravel, in which it lies in lumps, from one to fifty pounds weight. Under this strata is a sand rock, easily broken up with a pick-axe, and when exposed to the air, readily crumbles to fine sand. The ore intermixed in the sand rock is similar to that in the upper gravel strata. Under the sand rock is a strata of red clay about six feet thick. Beneath the clay is the best ore, in lumps from ten to two or three hundred pounds weight, the outside of which is frequently covered with a gold or silver coloured talky substance; some portion of arsenic and sulphur; and more or less of spar, antimony, and zinc, are sometimes found intermixed with the ore. Some of this ore will yield from sixty to seventy-five per cent.

About five miles from Barton's, in an eastern direction, is an old mine, discovered by the French, as early as their first settlement in this country, and was worked until Barton erected a furnace at his mine. It was then neglected until the year 1802, when a number of French families made a settlement near it. On opening the mine they found a rich ore in great plenty. But the French furnaces were very badly constructed. They were formed somewhat similar to a lime kiln, at the bottom of which they placed a flooring of large logs, and set up a tier of smaller ones around the sides of the furnace, within which they put a large quantity of ore. A fire was then made and continued until the mineral was smelted, and run off into troughs made to receive it ; but much of the metal was burnt up, or lost in the ashes. In this manner each family smelted their own mineral, until Mr. Austin erected nis furnace. Since that time, they find it more advantageous to sell ther ore to him. It is conjectured that the whole distance between the old mine and Barton's is one continued bed of lead ore.

The time of working the mines is from August to December. After the harvests are over, the inhabitants of Saint Genevieve and other settlements on the Mississippi resort to the mines. The rich employ their negroes, and the poor people work for themselves ; depending on the lead they procure, to furnish necessary articles for their families. The lead is estimated equal to cash for whatever they wish to purchase.

Another mine, called Ranalt's mine, situated on a creek of the same name about six miles north of Barton's, is said to contain very rich ore, but has been worked only a short time.

On another branch of the Marameg, are what are called the American mines, discovered by a number of Americans, who commenced a settlement near them. The appearance of the ore was very promising; but their title to the land has been contested by a number of Frenchmen, who have taken it from them, and have since made little progress in working the mineral.

La Plate mine is on a branch of the river known by that name, which was also discovered by some Americans. A large quantity of rich ore has been found near the surface, and appearances indicate a great extent of the mineral. Little, however, has yet been done in working of it.

At a few miles distant from La Plate, is Joe's mine. The ore is found in large bodies of several hundred pounds weight, and very pure and solid, but has not been much worked. At a small distance from this is Lany's mine, but the mineral is of little estimation. Several other mines have been discovered on the head waters of the Marameg, more than one hundred miles above Barton's of which very little is yet known.

La Motte's mine is on the waters of the St. Francis, about thirty miles S. W. from St. Genevieve. It was discovered and began to be worked about the year 1723. The mineral is very solid, disposed in regular veins of three or four feet in thickness. Five of these veins have been opened, and a part of them worked. They are found about four or five feet below the surface, and descend in an oblique direction, at an angle of about 45 degrees. They are in low, flat land, and in a very unhealthy situation; nor can the miners go down very deep before they will be interrupted by water. The mineral is very different in its appearance from any other that has been found in this part of the country. It is of a fine, steel grain, and contains a considerable quantity of silver. In smelting of it, a very different process is necessary from that which the French people have employed, in the other mines. The want of skilful workmen, and differently constructed furnaces, has greatly retarded the working of this mineral. The method these people have pursued, has been to give the ore repeated heatings, by laying it on piles of logs, before it is prepared for smelting, by which great loss is sustained. They rarely get more than thirty or thirty-five per cent.

There is also found, at this mine, a different kind of ore in beds. It is called, by the miners, gravel mineral, being found intermixed with the soil, in small particles, from the size of a pin's head to that of a hickory nut. After being washed, it is put into a furnace, and smelted into slag, and then placed in another furnace, not unlike a miller's hopper, where a partial fluxion is produced. It is said this kind of ore, in the hands of experienced workmen, with a proper furnace, would yield large profits.

Barton's mine, since the improvements made by Mr. Austin, is calculated to produce lead to the amount of twenty thousand dollars per annum. As the mineral is so easily obtained, the other mines, under proper management, might, doubtless, be rendered exceedingly profitable.

On the borders of the Mississippi, from Saint Genevieve to Cape Girardeau, there are scattered settlements and some considerable villages; but from the Cape to the mouth of the Ohio, there are very few settlers.

The face of the country in Upper Louisiana is somewhat broken, but the soil is generally fertile. " It is elevated and healthy, and well watered, with a variety of large rapid streams, calculated for mills and other water works. From Cape Girardeau, above the mouth of the Ohio, to the Missouri, the land contiguous to the river is generally much higher than on the east side, and in many places very rocky on the shore. Some of the heights exhibit a scene truly picturesque. They rise to a height of at least three hundred feet, faced with a perpendicular lime and free stone, carved into various shapes and figures by the hand of nature, and afford the appearance of a multitude of antique towers. From the tops of these elevations, the land gradually slopes back from the river, without gravel or rock, and is covered with valuable timber. It may be said with truth, that, for fertility of soil, no part of the world exceeds the borders of the Mississippi;

the land yields an abundance of all the necessaries of life, and almost spontaneously; very little labour being required in the cultivation of the earth. That part of Upper Louisiana, which borders on North Mexico, is one immense prairie; it produes nothing but grass; it is filled with buffaloe, deer, and other kinds of game; the land is represented as too rich for the growth of forest trees. It is pretended that upper Louisiana contains in its bowels many silver and copper mines, and various specimens of both are exhibited. Several trials have been made to ascertain the fact; but the want of skill in the artists has hitherto left the business undecided."*

The Mississippi, from the junction of the Missouri, has a strong current, which cannot be stemmed by the force of wind on sails, without the aid of oars. The width of the river is about one mile and a half, and the water always thick and muddy. A depth of fifteen feet of water can be carried down, in low stages of the river; but immediately below the Ohio it deepens to twenty-five feet, and still increases to sixty feet.

These waters are well replenished with fish of different kinds. The largest are the cat fish, the spatula fish, and sturgeon. The cat have been taken weighing more than one hundred pounds, and the spatula, of fifty pounds weight. The smaller fish are the pike, buffaloe, perch, trout,

* Appendix.—Ohio Navigator, page 138.

gar, mullet, and carp. It may, however, be doubted whether the carp be of the same species of those caught in Europe. It has been said that herring have been taken in these waters. Alligators have not been observed higher up than the Arkansas river. A peculiar kind of fresh water turtle abounds in these rivers. The feet are webbed, and the upper shell remarkably soft. They are from ten to fifteen pounds weight, and considered very delicious.

Fowl, the greater part of the year, are to be seen here in great abundance; such as swan, crane, heron, geese, ducks, and brant. The pelican are sometimes seen, but far down the river, are very numerous. The size and shape of this singular bird resembles the swan, excepting in its monstrous pouch which is placed under its neck and bill. It seems to be an appendage which nature has provided for carrying and preserving its food for its own support and that of its young. The pouch of a pelican killed by Captain Lewis, when ascending the Missouri, was found to hold five gallons of water. They are frequently prepared and used for bags and other purposes.

The forest trees, in Upper Louisiana, are generally similar to those in the State of Ohio and Indiana Territory. Black and white mulberry is found here in much greater plenty, especially on the Missouri. The cotton wood tree grows in great abundance, on the borders of these rivers. It has been supposed to be the same as the lombardy poplar, but it is probably a different species. It differs, at least, in the very large quantity of volatile, capillary pappus attached to the seeds. Wnen the seed vessels open, and the seeds come out, it almost fills the air, and, as it descends, covers the bushes and ground, like a fall of light snow. Its appearance very nearly resembles cotton wool, which has doubtless occasioned its trivial name.

The pecan, or Illinois hickery, grow plenty on the Mississippi. In the swamps and lowest flooded land, the cypress of a large size is the principal growth. Where the land is less inundated the swamp and live oak abound, which is highest estimated for ship building. The points at the bends of the river, and ends of islands, are chiefly covered with thickets of small willows.

At the confluence of the Ohio with the Mississippi, its width is very little increased, and continues generally about a mile and a half, as far as the Natchez, where it begins to grow somewhat broader. The principal rivers which discharge their waters into the Mississippi, are the Saint Francis, White, Arkansas, and Red river, on the western side, and on the eastern, the Wolf and the Yazoo rivers.

Immediately on passing out of the Ohio into the Mississippi, the current is very sensibly accelerated, but is not so strong as between the Ohio and the Missouri. It is estimated to run at the rate of three and a half to four miles an hour; and when the water is high is somewhat increased. The river is exceedingly serpentine, and the islands numerous. Some of the bends in its course down to the line of demarkation, are sudden and large; but between that line and Pointe Coupee, there are several of prodigious magnitude.

In navigating the Mississippi, there is at all times a sufficient depth of water, but many sand bars make off into the river. Frequent strong eddies, and many large currents of water, sitting out of the river, when the water is high, with great rapidity, require the constant and careful attention of the navigator. The navigation is also impeded and endangered, by what are called planters. These are large bodies of trees, with their roots fast at the bottom of the river, and stumps but just above the surface of the water. Another impediment is called sawyers, which are bodies of trees standing in a sloping manner, and moving up and down by the force of the current. A third inconvenience is small wooden islands, composed of drift wood, which, by some means, has been arrested, and immoveably fixed to the bottom; not rising much above the water, are to be seen only at a short distance.

Soon after entering the Mississippi from the Ohio, the whole prospect is so much changed, as to exhibit the appearance of a different country; the climate becomes mild and soft; and the cold of winter seems to have produced very little effect on the state of vegetation. The sameness of view along the banks of the river, as far down as Pointe Coupee, a distance of nine hundred miles, is scarcely interrupted, excepting by a few settlements, and some high bluffs, on the eastern side. The land appears to be one continued level, clothed with large timber, and an under growth of cane brakes, and small shrubs.

Opposite the mouth of the Ohio is a small settlement consisting principally of men whose employment is hunting. Five miles below, on the east side, is fort Jefferson, which is evacuated. On the west side, sixty-five miles further down, is New Madrid. This settlement was made by Col. George Morgan, of New Jersey, about the year 1790. It is pleasantly situated, on a rich soil, and was intended for a large town. After building a small number of houses, the people became extremely sickly, and no further progress was made in the settlement. On the same side, thirty-three miles below, in a bend of the river, is a settlement, two miles long, called Little Prairie. This tract of land is exceedingly rich and productive.

The first high lands to be seen on the river are the Chickasaw bluffs, on the eastern side. These bluffs are four in number, the first of which are one hundred and seventy-six miles below the Ohio, and continue about a mile on the river. The second are eleven miles below the first; the third twenty-one miles below the second, and extend about three quarters of a mile. Passing these bluffs, the river is extremely crooked. They rise from sixty to one hundred and fifty feet above the surface of the water. The fourth are thirty-three miles below the third, and just above them Wolf river enters from the eastward. The mouth of this river is not large, and contiguous to it is the site of fort Pike. These bluffs continue about two miles. On the lower extremity is fort Pickering, in an eligible and commanding situation, overlooking the whole of this elevated ground. When this fort was built, fort Pike was evacuated. It is a Captain's command, who has a detachment stationed at Post Ozark on the Arkansus river. This fort is in the Mississippi Territory, where the United States keep a Factor. Here is a small settlement of whites and Indians; but the most of these people are the half breed, which is a mixture of both of them.

On the western side, about sixty-five miles further down, comes in the river Saint Francis. Its mouth is about two hundred yards wide; the current is gentle; and is navigable for a considerable distance. The head waters of this river are said to be not far distant from Saint Genevieve, in a south westerly direction. At the entrance of the river, stood Kappas Old Fort, built by the French, principally for a magazine of stores and provisions, during their wars with the Chickasaw Indians.

Six miles below the Saint Francis, is a beautiful natural meadow, called the Big Prairie. At a small distance from the river, in this prairie, is a fine lake, five miles long, and three wide; it abounds with swan; and discharges its water into the river, by a large bayau.

About eighty-five miles below, enters White river on the same side; and about twenty miles further, comes in the Arkansas, which is much larger than White river; and admits of navigation to a great distance. A communication is made between these rivers by an inland channel, which goes out of White river about three miles above its mouth, and about twenty miles up the Arkansas, connecting the waters of the two rivers. The distance of the Post and Village of Ozark, on the Arkansas, is fifty miles from the mouth of that river; but by passing up White river, and through the channel, it is reduced to about thirty miles. On the upper and head waters of the Arkansas, are a large number of Indian villages.

Two hundred and ten miles below the Arkansas, the Yazoo river enters on the eastern side, which takes its rise in Georgia. It comes in with a gentle current, and is nearly three hundred yards wide. It abounds with swan, geese, ducks, and other water fowl. On the borders of this river are the much famed lands, purchased of the State of Georgia, and sold to New England speculators, called the Yazoo company. Twelve miles further down are Walnut hills; on the highest part of which, fort Henry was built, but has been long evacuated. Below Walnut hills, about twenty-four miles, commences the Palmira settlement, on the same side. This is a very handsome settlement; it contains a large number of houses; extends eight miles on the river; and is in a flourishing state. The land is very rich, and well improved in the culture of cotton. Further down about thirty miles, is the famous seat of Judge *Brain.* This house is pleasantly situated. This gentleman possesses a large and handsome farm, which is under excellent culture. He is much respected for his hospitality and politeness to passengers when they call upon him.

The city of Natchez is about one hundred and twenty miles below the Walnut hills. It is situated on an extremely elevated bank, which recedes back from the river, with a very moderate descent. Fronting the river, the bluff is nearly perpendicular, and two hundred feet in height, from the surface of the water. Between the base of the bluff and the river, is a space which is level, about six hundred feet wide; it is used for landing; and is spread over with dwellings, trading houses and shops. From this little village a road is dug out, in a zigzag form, to the summit of the bank. The city is built at some distance from the edge of the precipice, leaving a space for a handsome common. It contains more than three hundred houses, mostly frame, and one story high. Some of those more recently erected are two story, and in a handsome style. The houses generally are commodiously constructed for the transacting business, and the free admission of air in the hot season. The prospect from the city is delightful; commanding an extensive view of the river in both directions. There are two printing offices, issuing weekly papers; a post office, receiving a mail once a week; several mercantile houses, and a large number of smaller stores and shops. Great quantities of cotton, indigo, tobacco, and other commodities, are annually shipped from this city, where the accumulation of wealth is pursued with industry and ardour. It is a port of entry, and ships of four hundred tons can come up from Orleans, which is about three hundred miles, without any other obstruction than the strength of the current.

The land in the district of Natchez is generally rich and very productive. It is elevated ground, extending about one hundred and thirty miles on the Mississippi, and from twenty to thirty miles back from the river. Some parts of it are broken, by hills, which favours the raising of horses, neat cattle, sheep, and swine. In the woods and swamps they get their living during the winter. The wool of the sheep is not so good, being more hairy than in the country further north. Frequent changes in the state of the weather are experienced in the winter, but is rarely excessive hot in the summer.

Cotton is the staple commodity, and is raised in great perfection; it is planted the last of February, or beginning of March. Those who have large plantations derive great profits, and are able, in a short time, to accumulate handsome fortunes. This is the utmost northern limits of the growth of the sugar cane. Some sugar has been made, but this kind of culture does not succeed. Excellent Indian corn is produced with little labour, and may be planted from the first of March to July. Good rye has grown in some ground, but wheat does not succeed. Indigo, hemp, flax, and rice, are cultivated to advantage. Apples and cherries appear not to be adapted to the climate, but plumbs, peaches, figs, and olives, yield their fruit in plenty. Sweet and sour oranges will grow here, but thrive much better further down the river.

About fifty miles below Natchez are Loftus' Heights. Fort Adams is on the side of these heights, about one third of the way up, and on the summit is a strong block house, which overlooks the fort and surrounding country. A Captain's command is stationed at the fort; and four miles east, at Washington Springs, is a handsome cantonment, with quarters for three hundred men. On the land in this vicinity are considerable settlements.

Four miles below Fort Adams, is the line of demarkation, agreed upon between the United States and the Spanish government. Prior to the purchase of Louisiana, this line was the boundary of the United States, on the south.

At a small distance below the line, the river turns short and forms a large bend to the westward. At the extremity of this curve, Red river enters the Mississippi, on the west side. This river is large, and extends far into the country in a northwesterly direction. On the banks and vicinity of this river are the thriving and populous settlement of Rapide, Avoyelles, and Natchitoches. This river is used to communicate with the frontiers of New Mexico. Three miles below Red river, on this bend, the bayau Chaffalio runs out with a great rapidity, and is the first large river which leaves the Mississippi, and falls by a separate channel into the Gulf of Mexico. Although there is a sufficient depth of water, the navigation is prevented by a prodigious quantity of drift wood, which has formed a floating bridge across it, of several miles in length. This bridge, in some places, is said to be so compact and firm, that horses and cattle are driven over it. These obstructions are constantly accumulating by the trees and rubbish which are passing into this stream from the Mississippi.

The great bend is continued below the bayau Chaffalio, until it forms a semicircle; the river then tends to the southward some distance, where it winds round to the eastward and northward, and runs back in a direction nearly opposite to its general course, until it comes within five or six miles of the line of demarkation, just below which the great bend first commenced. The distance across the land is only five miles, called the Short Cut; but following the course of the river is fifty miles. Here the bend still continues, turning to the eastward and southward, until it comes within one mile and a half of the river in its course to the northward; nearly completing a circle of about thirty miles in circumference. The last of these bends is called Tunica Bend, at the extremity of which is Tunica village, a handsome settlement, extending about twelve miles along the east side of the river.

Point Coupee is about fifteen miles below Tunica village, on the western side, where there was formerly a bend, nearly resembling Tunica Bend, but of smaller size. Here the river, after making a circuit of about twenty miles, returned almost into its own stream. A channel, some years ago, was cut across, and by the washing of the current, the river is become as deep and broad as it is above and below, by which a saving is made of about twenty miles in the distance. The old bend is called Fausse Riviere.

Point Coupee is a rich and populous settlement, extending about twenty miles on the river. The land is laid out in beautiful cotton plantations, producing great crops. Here commences the embankment or Levee, on the western side of the river, which is continued to Orleans, a distance of about one hundred and seventy miles. Here the beauty of the Mississippi and prospect of the country exhibit a view so enchantingly delightful, as scarcely to admit of description. On the side of this elevated, artificial bank, is a range of handsome, neatly built houses, appearing like one continued village, as far as the city of Orleans. They are one story, framed buildings, elevated on piles six or eight feet high, and well painted ; the paint generally white. The houses for the slaves are mostly placed on straight lines and nicely white-washed. The perpetual verdure of numerous orange trees, intermixed with fig trees surrounding the houses, and planted in groves and orchards near them, highly beautify the prospect; while the grateful fragrance of constant blossoms, and the successive progress to plentiful ripened fruit, charm the eye, and regale the senses.

Baton Rouge, a very fine, flourishing settlement, is about thirty miles below Point Coupee, on the eastern side of the river. Here the high lands terminate in an elevated bluff, thirty or forty feet above the greatest rise of the water in the river And here commences the embankment or Levee, which is continued, like that on the western side, to Orleans ; and a range of houses, ornamented with orange and fig trees, the same distance, perfectly similar to that on the opposite bank. Baton Rouge settlement extends about twenty miles on the river, and to a considerable distance back, in an eastern direction. The soil is rich; the cotton plantations are well cultivated, producing plentiful crops.

About fifteen miles further down, on the same side, is the river Iberville, which forms an outlet from the Mississippi when the water is high, but when the river is low, it is dry. The water of this stream runs into the lakes Maurepas and Ponchartrain, and through them to the sea, forming what is called the island of New Orleans. At a point a little below the Iberville, commences an uninterrupted series of plantations, which are continued, upwards of one hundred miles, to the city of Orleans. These plantations are all cleared in front, and under improvement. Some of them are planted with sugar cane, but the greater part with cotton. They are narrow at the bank, and extend back to the swampy ground, which is incapable of cultivation; the land no where admitting of more than one plantation deep.

At the point below the Iberville, the Mississippi turns short to the westward, forming a large bend. At the extremity of this bend is an outlet, called the bayau Placquemine, on the western side, discharging its waters into the sea. By this bayau is the principal communication with the two populous and rich settlements of Atacapas and Opelousas. These settlements are the most wealthy in Louisiana, abounding in horses and neat cattle; containing a large quantity of good land, capable of being much better improved.

The bayau la Fourche, on the same side, is about thirty miles further down, following the meanders of the river, and eighty from the city of Orleans. From this bayau the course of the river is nearly south east, and much more direct to the city. Bayau la Fourche is a large outlet, forming a considerable river, which communicates with the sea to the west of the Balise. In old maps it is called La Riviere des Chetamaches. When the water is high it will admit of craft of sixty or seventy tons burden. On its banks are numerous settlements, one plantation deep. The land is rich and gradually descends from the banks to the swamps, which are generally covered with water, and incapable of cultivation. The culture is principally cotton.

From this outlet to the city, the land will admit of only one plantation deep, and is rarely capable of cultivation, more than one mile from the bank of the river. It then becomes low and swampy to the lakes and the sea. The swamps are immense, intersected by creeks and lakes, extending more than one hundred miles to the high lands of Atacapas. But the swamps generally abound with large cypress trees. Great quantities of this timber is sawed by mills, erected on streams formed by cutting sluices through the Levee. These mills are worked with great rapidity nearly half the year. What has been said of the situation, soil, and culture of the plantation below Iberville, on the eastern side of the river, will very nearly apply to those which are opposite, on the western side.

The city of New Orleans, is situated in a bend of the river, on the eastern side, in latitude thirty, north, and longitude ninety, west. It was laid out by the French, in the year 1720, extending about a mile on front, from the gate of France, to that of Chapitoulas, and somewhat more than one third of a mile in rear to the rampart. On the upper side an extensive suburb has been added, called Saint Mary. The streets are straight, crossing each other at right angles, but are much too narrow, being only thirty-two French feet in width. In the centre of the front of the city is a large, handsome square, called *Place D'armes*. The church and town house, built of stone, stand facing the square. The houses in front of the city, and one or two squares back, are mostly brick, and are two stories high; the rest of the houses are chiefly one story, and built of wood. They are elevated about eight feet from the ground, to avoid the inconvenience of water, and the under part generally occupied as cellars. The city has been fortified, but the works, which were originally too deficient to have been defended, have gone to decay, and are now principally removed. There are about one thousand five hundred houses, and between ten and twelve thousand inhabitants, including Saint Mary's. It is the capital of Louisiana, and the seat of government of the lower territory. Although the situation is unhealthy, large accessions to the population are annually made from the United States, and from other parts of the world. It is the principal mart of the western country, where large shipments are made to foreign markets. From its local advantages, it bids fair to become one of our greatest commercial cities.

Opposite to the city, the river is about one mile and a half in breadth, running with a pretty strong current; and yet there is a perceptible rise of the tide; when the water is low it ebbs and flows from a foot to a foot and a half, in perpendicular height. The distance from the city to the sea, at the mouth of the river, is about one hundred and eight miles; and the country low and swampy, containing very little land capable of cultivation. Fifteen miles below the city, and at the head of the English bend, is a settlement, called Saint Bernardo, or Terre aux Bœuf, containing two parishes. The inhabitants are nearly all Spaniards from the Canaries, who improve a narrow strip of land, principally for raising poultry and garden vegetables, for the market at New Orleans. At this place a cantonment was formed, and the late army, under the command of General Wilkinson, was mostly stationed, where a very distressing and mortal sickness prevailed among the troops.

From this settlement to the fort of Plaquemines, forty-eight miles, the land is a morass, almost impassable for man or beast, and always overflowed for several months in the year, but filled with cypress and jack brush. From Plaquemines to the Passes is twenty-four miles, where the river branches into three parts. These branches are called Passes, and distinguished, by the east, south, and west Pass. The land in this distance is mostly clothed with jack bushes and tall weeds. From these branches to the sea is about twenty miles, and the land has the appearance of a vastly extended marsh, destitute of trees or shrubs, but covered with long grass.

The East Pass, at the distance of six miles, divides into two branches. The eastern is called Pass a la Loutre, and the other Belize. On the Belize is a small black house, called by the same name, and near it are a number of houses, occupied by pilots. Large ships, bound up the river, enter it by this Pass; there being the greatest depth of water on the bar. At the entrance of this Pass about sixteen feet of water may be carried over the bar. The bars lie without the mouths of the Passes, are very narrow, and immediately after passing them the water deepens to six or seven fathoms. The South Pass, which is directly in front of Mississippi, has been almost entirely choaked with drift wood, but has about ten feet of water on the bar. The West Pass, which is the longest and narrowest, and used to be the passage by which large ships entered the river, had some years ago eighteen feet, but is now said to be reduced to only eight feet of water on the bar.

The productions of Louisiana are cotton, sugar, rum, indigo, rice, corn, furs, and peltry. It also affords lumber, tar, pitch, lead, horses, and cattle. The fertility of the soil admits of great increase of these and an additional supply of many other articles. The culture of the sugar cane, which has already become considerable, may doubtless be carried to a very great extent. At present, cotton is the largest and most profitable production. Indigo is on the decline. Further north than the Iberville, the sugar cane is liable to be injured by the cold, and the crops rendered uncertain; but all the lands southward, susceptible of improvement, and adapted to that kind of culture, will produce the cane in good perfection. In some parts it is already became a staple commodity. Some planters employ about one quarter of their plantations in the production of sugar cane, and the remainder in pasture, and raising provisions. It is estimated that one hundred and eighty feet square will produce, on an average, twelve hundred weight of sugar, and fifty gallons of rum. Calculating on this data, it is presumed the lands under present cultivation, suited to this culture, would produce about fifty thousand hogsheads of sugar, and twenty-four thousand puncheons of rum. It is believed by some, that as a full and regular supply of provisions may be easily obtained from above, on moderate terms, one half the arable land might be planted with cane, to advantage. It is likewise an undoubted fact, that large portions of vacant land are to be found, well adapted to the culture of the cane. The following quantities of sugar, brown, clayed, and refined, were imported into the United States from Louisiana and the Floridas, viz. in the year 1799—773,542 pounds ; in the year 1800—1,560,887 pounds ; in the year 1801—967,619 pounds, and in the year 1802—1,576,993 pounds. The quantity produced in the succeeding years has probably been considerably increased.

A TOPOGRAPHICAL DESCRIPTION

OF

RED RIVER.

This river enters the Mississippi on the western side, at the first great bend below Fort Adams, about nine miles distant from the crossing of the line of demarkation. It is large, and one of the most beautiful rivers in Lower Louisiana. Its waters are brackish, of a reddish colour, turbid, and deposit a sediment collected from the red banks, far up the river. The banks are overflowed in the spring to a great extent, and in places to the depth of fifteen or eighteen feet. The freshets begin to fall in June, and by August the water retires to the channel of the river and lagoons. In the low lands the growth is principally willow and cotton wood, and on the higher, large elms, ash, and hickory; where the grape vine greatly abounds. About six miles from the mouth of the river is a bayau, leading from Lake Long, which is a narrow lake, two or three miles in width, and fourteen or fifteen in length. Twenty-five miles further up is the confluence of Black river, which is large at its mouth, and coming from a northerly direction.

The first settlement on Red river, called *Baker's* station, at the commencement of Avoyelles is about seventy miles from its mouth, as the river runs, although not more than one third of the distance, on a straight course. Above this station is a prairie thirty or forty miles in circumference. It is entirely destitute of trees or shrubs, but produces an excellent grass for fattening cattle. The beef is said to be of an excellent quality, and hogs find ground nuts and other food, on which they thrive, and become good pork. The inhabitants are settled in the outer skirts, on the border of the woods. This prairie has the appearance of a good soil, but is found to be too cold for cotton and Indian corn, which thrive much better on land where there has been a growth of wood. Little or no wheat is raised, as they have no mills to grind it. The inhabitants are a mixture of Spaniard, French, Irish, and Americans, who are generally poor, and extremely ignorant.

A few miles above this prairie, the land begins to be moderately hilly. Near the river, the timber is oak, hickory, and some pine, but back from the river the growth is mostly pine for thirty or forty miles.

Holmes' station is about forty miles above Baker's, where there is a settlement. The land produces good cotton, corn, and tobacco. On the south side of the river there is a large body of rich land, extending to Appalousa, which is watered and drained by two large bayaus, called bayau Robert and bayau Beuf. Their waters are very clear, and take their rise in the high lands betwen Red river and the Sabine. These waters are discharged into the Chaffetis. It is believed this body of land, which is forty miles square, in richness of soil, growth of timber, goodness of water, and convenience of navigation is equal to any tract of land in this part of Louisiana.

From *Holmes'* to bayau Rapide is thirty-five miles, and for this distance there are only a few scattered settlements on the right side of the river, and none on the left. The right side is preferred on account of the high lands, which are most convenient for keeping stock. The lands on the bayau Rapide, are nearly of the same quality with the bayau Robert and bayau Beuf. The two mouths of this bayau meet the river about twenty miles apart. The length of this bayau is about thirty miles, forming a curvature somewhat in the shape of a half moon. On its back another bayau falls into it, of excellent water, on which there is a saw mill. Boats cannot pass round this curvature on the account of obstructions formed by rafts of timber, but can ascend from the lower mouth more than half the distance. On each side the lower mouth is the principal settlement, called the Rapide settlement,

Few countries exhibit a more delightful appearance than this settlement. The plantations are extremely beautiful, and the soil exceedingly rich. The cotton raised here is of the best quality in Louisiana. The corn and tobacco are very good, as are all kinds of vegetables. The orange and fig trees grow luxuriously, and the climate is delightful.

At the Rapide is a fall of water, occasioned by a soft rock which crosses the bed of the river, so that from July to December there is not sufficient water for boats to pass over, but the rest of the season they pass with ease. This rock is so very soft, as not much to exceed, in hardness, some kinds of hard clay, and it is presumed a passage might be cut through it, with very little difficulty, so as to make it as low as the bed of the river.

From the Rapide to the Indian villages is about twenty miles, with very few settlements for the whole distance, although the land is fine, and susceptible of all kind of cultivation. The Indian villages are pleasantly situated on both sides of the river, and the land very good. Just above these villages is *Gillard's* station, on an high pine bluff, which, on the east side, overlooks extensive fields and meadows, in a good state of cultivation, and affords a view of a very long reach of the river. Here is an excellent spring of water, gushing out from an aperture in a rock on the bank of the river, about high water mark. Back from the house is a lake, which abounds with fish in summer, and fowl in the winter.

About six miles above *Gillard's* is the village of the Boluxa Indians, where the river divides into two branches, forming an island of about fifty miles in length, and three or four in breadth. The right hand stream is called *Rigula de Bondieu*, on which there are no settlements. On the left hand is the boat channel to Natchitoches, and on this branch, for twenty-four miles, there are thick settlements, and the inhabitants wealthy. This is called the River Cane settlement.

Above this settlement, the river divides again, forming another Island of about thirty miles in length, and three or four in breadth, called *Isle Brevel*. This Island is subdivided by a bayau which crosses the Island from one river to the other, and is called Bayau Brevel. The middle division of the river is called Little river, and is the boat channel, where there are thick settlements. The westward channel, called False river, is navigable, but the banks being very low, there are no settlements. The river passes through a lake, called *Lai Occasse*. Above this lake the three channels meet, where Natchitoches is situated. The town is small, and meanly built, containing about forty or fifty houses, inhabited principally by French people.

The fort, which is now called Fort Claiborn, is on a small hill, forty rods from the river, containing about two acres. This hill is wholly occupied by the fort and barracks, and is elevated thirty feet above the river banks. Natchitoches is an ancient French settlement, which commenced nearly a century ago, where a trading post was established, and an extensive traffic carried on with the Indians. This despicable village is not on the site where the ancient town stood ; the present inhabitants, having been almost entirely secluded from the civilized world, have degenerated to a miserable, ignorant set of beings ; but a small degree removed from the state of the savages, with whom they have had their principal intercourse. When a large trade was carried on with the natives, many years ago, the town was much larger than it is at present; the people having left the town to settle on farms in the adjacent country, but principally on the long round, near the river. Very little now remains to be seen of the old parts of the town, except the form of their gardens, and a few ornamental trees. There is one great inconvenience in settling near Red river; the waters being never clear, and always brackish. Wells, sunk near the river, have brackish and unpleasant water. There are some tolerable springs, but the inhabitants are obliged principally to depend on rain water.

Near Natchitoches are two large lakes, one a mile, and the other six miles distant. One of the lakes is thirty, and the other fifty or sixty miles in circumference. These lakes are connected with the river by bayaus. When the water rises in the river, it rushes into the lakes, and then rushes back again, as the water falls in the river. The immense number of fowl which abound in these lakes, during the winter, almost exceeds credibility. The air is darkened with the large flights, especially near the close of the day ; and the ear almost stunned with the noise they make. One man may kill many hundreds in an afternoon. The hunter takes his station on a convenient spot, and loads and fires as fast as possible, without taking particular aim, until he finds he has killed a sufficient number to load his horses. These fowl are swan, geese, brant, and several species of ducks. In the summer, several kinds of fish are said to be equally plenty. The Indians, in taking fish, frequently make use only of the bow and arrow. With this instrument an Indian will often load his horse in a very short time. The fish consist principally of the cat, pike, buffaloe, sucker, and white and black perch, and are generally of a very large size.

From Natchitoches there is a communication with the frontiers of New Mexico. Here the road leading to Saint a Fé leaves Red river, and passes, in a westerly direction through the Spanish Province of Texes. The country is said to consist of very extensive plains, abounding with horses and cattle. Major Z. M. Pike, who was sent, by the government to explore the head waters of the Osage and Red river, was taken by the Spaniards, and he and his party, as prisoners, were conducted to Saint a Fé. He found the city large and populous; the country thickly settled, and highly cultivated. When he was liberated, he was conducted, on his return to the United States, in a different route, through a country well filled with inhabitants and a number of large cities.

At the distance of about ten miles above Natchitoches, there is another lake which is on the northeast side of Red river, called *Noiz*, and is about fifty miles in circumference. The bayau or outlet of this lake communicates with Rigula de Bondieu. The bayau Rigula de Bondieu enters Red river about three miles above Natchitoches. Near the lake Noiz, all the salt used on Red river is made. This large quantity of salt, until lately, was made by only two men, and with a few pots and kettels. It is now better worked, but not to a hundredth part of the extent to which it might be carried. The water is so highly impregnated with salt as to require very little boiling. The conveyance of the salt to market is easy, as the bayau is boatable most of the year into the lake.

Where the bayau communicates, Red river is in one channel, and here the settlement of Grand Ecore commences, extending about six miles. Stone coal is found near this settlement, and some fine springs of water issue from the banks of the river. About one mile above Grand Ecore, on the left side of the river comes in a large bayau from the *Spanish lake,* so called. This lake is about fifty miles in circumference, and rises and falls with the river, in the same manner as the lakes near Natchitoches. Two miles above this bayau the river is divided into two streams. The course of the west branch is westerly for nearly eighty miles, where it turns to the eastward, and communicates with the right branch, forming an Island one hundred miles long, and in some parts of it thirty miles wide. The upper end of this branch is so choaked up with drift wood that boats cannot pass. Settlements, of entirely French people, extend nearly the whole length of this branch, called bayau Peir settlements. The land is fertile, and the scattered inhabitants possess large herds of cattle, and appear to live very well. The face of this tract of country is moderately hilly, and the water very good. Some miles westward, towards the Sabine river, is a saline, where they procure their salt.

On the main, or eastern branch of the river, there are a few scattered settlements, including one called Camti. The land on this branch is similar to that on the other, excepting that near Camti, it is much intersected and broken by bayaus. The land at the upper part of these settlements is considered not inferior to any on the Red river. The computed distance from the mouth of Red river is one hundred and forty miles, and between thirty and forty from Natchitoches. At the upper houses the great jam of drifted timber begins, choaking up the river, at intermediate places, which are frequently several leagues apart, for one hundred miles. The stream is extremely crooked, and the low lands, which are rich, extend to a great width on each side. Although the river is so obstructed, boats of any size can ascend in a bayau most of the year. This is called bayau *Channo*, leading into lake *Biftino*, at the distance of about three miles from where it leaves the river. This lake is about sixty miles in length, and is nearly parallel with the river. A communication with the river is formed at the upper end, by a bayau, called *Daichet*. This passage is much shorter than to follow the meanders of the river. From this bayau to the mountains the river is free of obstructions.

Nearly eighty miles above bayau Daichet is the Caddo old town. The lands for this distance are rich, consisting of high bottom, which is widely extended from the river. The Caddo old towns consist of a number of villages built on a large prairie, in the midst of which is a lake of about five miles in circumference, without any stream running in, or out of it. The water is so perfectly limpid, and the bottom so clear, that the fish may be distinctly seen, at the depth of fifteen or twenty feet. On this prairie, and not far from the lake, is an eminence to which the Indians pay great veneration. They have a tradition, that the Great Spirit, having determined

CABREE

or Missouri ANTELOPE

to deluge the earth with water, and drown all the people upon it, selected one Caddo family, and placed it on this eminence. The water not rising so high as the top of it, this family was saved, when all the rest of the people in the world were destroyed; and from this family all the Indian nations are descendants. Not only the Caddos, but all the other bands of Indians, pay homage to this eminence, when they pass it. The neighbouring bands consider the Caddoquies their common father, and treat them with respect. Their number of warriors do not much exceed one hundred men, but they brave death with the utmost fortitude, and boast that they have never embrued their hands in the blood of a white man. They carry on an incessant warfare with the Osage and Chicktaw nations, but live in peace with the other bands.

From the Caddo old towns to the Panis villages, following the course of the river, which is nearly west, is about seven hundred miles; the land alternately clothed with timber and prairie, and some of the prairies very extensive. On a branch of Red river, which comes in about one hundred and thirty miles below the Panis towns, it is said, silver mines have been lately discovered; and just below the first village, the Ra-ha-cha-ha, or the Missouri branch of Red river, enters from the north; which is a large stream, and the water so brackish, that it cannot be drank. At its head waters, the Indians collect large lumps of rock salt. From the Panis villages to the head of Red river the land is broken and mountainous, and wholly destitute of wood, excepting willows and small cotton wood trees on the borders of the streams. The Indians report that there are many silver mines among these mountains, of which the white people have no knowledge.

The Panis or Towiache Indians, who reside on these waters, were once powerful, but are reduced to about four hundred warriors. They live in villages, and have large numbers of horses and mules, and raise corn, tobacco, beans, squashes, and pumpkins. They cut the pumpkins into long, narrow strips, as is sometimes done by white people, to dry them. When they are sufficiently wilted to be tough, they weave them into mats. These mats, with the other productions they raise, they sell to the roving bands of the Hietan Indians, who rove in the plains and mountains between Red river and Saint a Fé, but never live in villages. The Hietans wear these mats over their shoulders; and, as they travel, cut off pieces and eat, until they have devoured their mats. These commodities the Panis exchange for buffaloe robes, horses, and mules. Although their country abounds with game, they are not esteemed good hunters. Having few guns, they depend on their bows and arrows. The buffaloe, deer, bear, antelope, and wild hogs, are in great plenty; but they live principally on buffaloe meat, and rarely kill a deer. The men go naked, except their breech flap, and the women wear only a short coat of dressed leather, tied round the waist. These Indians are at perpetual war with the Osage nation.

Black river, a large branch of Red river, has already been mentioned. Coming from a northern direction, it enters Red river about thirty miles above its mouth. The course of Black river is nearly parallel with Mississippi, at a distance of about forty miles. Between these rivers the land is overflowed when the Mississippi is high. At the time this immense cypress swamp is flooded, it exhibits the appearance of a vast number of large trees, standing in a lake, or a bay of the sea. The name of black river, at the distance of sixty miles, is changed, and it is then called the Washata river. Here the course of the river tends to the westward, and the land becomes sufficiently high to admit of cultivation near the bank of the river. At the mouth of the Washata, and near lake Cattahoola, is a small settlement, where the settlers have raised an embankment to prevent inundation when the water is high. Above this settlement, at the distance of about one hundred and seventy miles, is an excellent tract of land, extending on the river, about forty miles. Here the much famed Aaron Burr pretended to have made an extensive purchase; to commence the settlement was the ostensible object for which he raised his army, and descended the Mississippi. After his progress was arrested, it is said, a small number of his men went into the ground, but remained only a short time. This tract is high prairie, interspersed with wood land; the soil is exceedingly rich, and the face of the county delightful. Some few settlements have been made upon it, and are extended still further up, where there is a small fort.

But the people are extremely indolent, and having contracted the habits of the Indians, had rather hunt than cultivate the soil. At the head waters of the Washata are the famous hot springs, of which much has been said, which, with many, exceeds credibility. It is asserted by those who have visited them, that meat held in them a short time will be sufficiently cooked for eating. The land where they are found is barren, hilly, and broken, but there are no volcanic appearances. Loud explosions are frequently heard among the hills, somewhat resembling the blowing of rocks with gun powder. These noises, the Indians say, are made by the spirits of white people, working in the hills, in search of silver and gold mines.

Between the heads of branches which enter Red river, and those which run into the Arkansas, is a range of high and impassable mountains, which extend to the great prairies, eastward of the waters of the Osage river. It is said, a gold mine has been discovered north of these mountains, on a branch of the Arkansas river. Indians and hunters likewise report, that in these mountains there are several silver mines.

It has been already mentioned, that Ozark Post and village is on the Arkansas, fifty miles above its mouth. At this post an Ensign's command is stationed, which is a detachment from the Captain's company, at Fort Pickering. The village contains about sixty families, chiefly hunters and traders; many of them the mixed breed of Indian and white, and all of them intolerably lazy and indolent. But the soil is exceedingly rich, producing every thing committed to it in great luxuriance. Twelve miles above this station is the village of Ozark, or Arkansas Indians, and six miles further are two more large villages. Their warriors are computed at one hundred and thirty, and about seven hundred inhabitants. They are friendly to all nations, except the Osage. Although they speak the same language, they are at perpetual war with each other. There are some smaller villages father up; and at the distance of about forty or fifty miles, the hills begin to rise on the south side; and about three hundred miles further, they become lofty, inaccessible mountains.

On the head waters of the Arkansas, a band of Osage Indians reside, who have separated from that nation on the Osage river. Their village is large, and their hunting ground a most excellent

10*

tract of high prairie, interspersed with groves of timber. It has a deep, rich soil, and abounds with a great variety of wild game. They are enemies to all the other nations except the little Osage band; none venture to settle near them, or presume to enter upon their hunting ground. The ridge of mountains between Arkansas and Red river, form a barrier to the Caddos, and the small nations who rised on those waters; but they sometimes make excursions round the mountains, and descend Red river, spreading terror and depredation among those tribes.

The widely extended, tributary streams of Red river, Arkansas, and Osage, extend into, and water an immense tract of country; and some of the branches of these rivers nearly interlock with each other. The head waters of the Osage river take their rise at no great distance from those of Red river. The general course of the Osage is nearly north, which, after running through, perhaps, the finest tract of country, east of the rocky mountains, for more than six hundred miles, enters the Missouri river, about two hundred miles above its mouth.

The immensely extended prairies commence about forty or fifty miles above the mouth of the Osage, on the western side. They generally approach to a level, but in some parts rise into swelling hills, destitute of wood; in some parts are small copses of wood; in others, forests of considerable extent; and usually the streams of water are bordered with a large growth. On some of the streams, the beautiful wood called *Bois jaun*, or *yellow wood*, has been found.

The Osage nation of Indians reside principally on this river. Their first villages commence about two hundred miles from its mouth. They are divided into two parties, called the Little and Great Osage, and live in different villages. The Little Osage nation, although derived from the Great Osage, formerly lived in villages at the mouth of Grand river, on the Missouri; but being exceedingly harrassed by the Sioux, and other tribes, removed up the Osage river, and placed themselves under the protection of the Great Osage. Their villages are the first, in ascending the river, and at a small distance beyond them, commences the villages of the Great Osage.

The Osage nation is one of the largest and most formidable, which has yet been discovered in these western regions. Their warriors, including the Little and Great Osage, are computed to amount to two thousand, and about eight thousand souls. They are remarkably tall, large, and ferocious. They are erect, well proportioned, and many of them measure six feet and two or three inches. They are expert hunters, and considered the best warriors in the western country. Being constantly at war with every tribe, without distinction, their very name carries terror with it into every other nation. They are generally equally inimical to white people, which has been often witnessed by their attacks on the settlements at Saint Louis, the lead mines, and Saint Genevieve. They never fall upon these settlements without making great depredations, and mostly get off without suffering much injury themselves. But the traders, when they have once entered their villages, are perfectly safe, and are treated with much respect and hospitality while there. Sometimes, however, in going and returning, they will fall upon, and rob them.

Although they are great hunters and distinguished warriors, and often ramble far in these excursions, they live in villages, and raise corn, beans, squashes, pumpkins, and melons. They are proud and overbearing, viewing all other nations with contempt. In their war expeditions, they are courageous, patient, and persevering; enduring great fatigue and hardship with the utmost fortitude. They delight so much in blood, that no sufferings are too great to encounter, if it be necessary in making their attacks upon their enemy by surprise. They generally kill all their prisoners, except the children; and these they will sometimes adopt as their own. No nation has been so able to withstand them, as the roving bands of the Sioux. Having no settled villages, they are always prepared for war, and encounter their enemy to more advantage. They sometimes engage in offensive wars, and venture to make attacks on the Osage villages.

The complexion of the Osage nation is between an olive and copper colour; their eyes dark brown; their noses large and aquiline, and their hair black, straight, and course. The men pluck out, or shave off, all the hair upon their heads, except a lock upon the crown, which they permit to grow its full length. They sometimes perforate the cartilage of the nose, in which they hang a drop, similar to an ear drop, and bore their ears nearly round to the top, in which they place a large number of silver ear-rings. They wear a breech flap fastened around the waist with a belt; a pair of leggins, and shoes or moccasons. These are made of dressed buffaloe or deer skin, and fancifully worked and ornamented with lead and porcupine quills, stained with different colours. A buffaloe robe, which is the skin dressed with the hair on, is worn over the shoulders, and serves for a cloak by day, and for a bed and covering by night. In the summer this robe is laid by, and they go naked, except the breech flap and leggins.

The women are large and well proportioned, rather inclined to corpulency; their faces oval; cheek bones somewhat high; but the features are regular, and not destitute of beauty. Their under garment is dressed leather, silk, or calico, without sleeves, and coming down below the knees. About the neck it is decorated with a large number of silver brooches. Their leggins and moccasons are similar to those of the men. Their hair is long, and neatly tied up, forming a club behind. Broad silver clasps are worn on their arms, wrists and ankles. They also, like the men, wear a buffaloe robe.

Their villages are built along the banks of the river. The houses stand in two rows, on a straight line, with a wide street between them. They build their houses with split logs, laid up in a neat manner, and cover them with split boards. They are generally about ten or twelve feet wide, and from twenty to forty feet long; and some of the chiefs have them sixty feet in length. The height is from eight to ten feet; and having no window or chimney, they have an aperture at the top for the light to come in, and the smoke to go out. They have only one door, which is usually closed with a buffaloe skin. These people live in a more neat and cleanly manner than is common among these western tribes.

The Osage nation claim an extensive country for their hunting ground, and do not admit the other nations to make encroachments upon it. It abounds with all the wild game common to this country; such as the elk, buffaloe, dear, bear, wolf, cabree, or antelope, ground hog, beaver, otter, and mink.

The title of their chiefs is hereditary. The great chief assumes authority over those of an inferior grade; and his power in many respects is dispotic. But he dare not engage in any great enterprize, nor make war or peace, without calling a council of the subordinate chiefs and warriors. To this council he states his object, and explains his views and intentions; and if a general assent be not given, he lays aside his project.

These people believe in a supreme power, whom they call the *Great Spirit*. To him they attribute every good they enjoy, and consider it as his gift. But they render homage to another Spirit, subordinate to the *Great Spirit*, who is the author of all the evil and misfortune they suffer. By appeasing his wrath, they hope to escape the troubles with which he might be disposed to visit them. They have also many other inferior deities, which they conceive have power to do them good or evil. They believe, if they are faithful to their nation and kind to their relatives, good warriors and good hunters, that when they die, they shall go to a most delightful country, which abounds in game; where there will be perpetual day; a bright sun and clear sky; when they will meet their old friends; and where they will enjoy every pleasure they were fond of here, without interruption. But that those who are bad here, especially those who are ungrateful to the aged, when they die, will go to a place of punishment, where they will suffer the severest privations, and be denied every thing that was pleasant or desirable in this life. But the traders say, it is with great difficulty they can be prevailed upon to converse at all on these subjects. The French made repeated attempts to introduce Missionaries among them, but could not succeed. There is said to be one remarkable trait in the character of the Osage Indians, in which they differ, perhaps, from all other tribes; they are extremely averse to ardent spirit, and few of them can be persuaded to taste it.

Below the Great Osage, on the waters of the Little Osage, Saint Francis and other streams, are a number of scattered bands of Indians, and two or three considerable villages. These bands were principally Indians, who were formerly outcasts from the tribes east of the Mississippi. Numbers have since joined from the Delawares, Shawanoes, Wayondott and other tribes towards the lakes. Their warriors are said to be five or six hundred. They have sometimes made excursions and done mischief on the Ohio river, but the settlements, on the Mississippi have suffered the most severely by their depredations.

A

CONCISE ACCOUNT

OF THE

INDIAN NATIONS,

WEST OF THE MISSISSIPPI, TO THE ROCKY

MOUNTAINS.

Little has been known of these nations until very lately. The following information is principally derived from the accounts given of them by Captain Lewis, when on his tour to the western ocean, communicated to the President of the United States; and by Dr. John Sibley, in his communications, from Natchetoches, to the Secretary of war. The advantages these gentlemen possessed for obtaining knowledge of their names, situations, numbers, and other circumstances respecting them, have been better than those of any others; and their accounts are undoubtedly the best that can at present be obtained.

The Osage nation has already been described. The nation residing next to the Osage, on the waters of the Missouri, is the Kanzas. Their village is on the Kanzas river, about eighty leagues from its mouth. This river comes from the south, meanders, for a great distance, through a fine, rich country, and is two hundred and fifty yards wide, where it enters the Missouri. The Kanzas have about three hundred warriors and thirteen hundred souls. They are commonly at war with all nations, except the Ottoes, with whom they have intermarriages. The limits of the country they claim is unknown; they hunt on the upper part of the Kanzas and Arkansas rivers. They live in their villages, from about the fifteenth of March to fifteenth of May, and again from the fifteenth of August to the fifteenth of October; the rest of the year they devote to hunting. At present, they are a dissolute, lawless, banditti; frequently plundering traders, and committing depredation on people ascending and descending the Missouri.

The Missouri nation live on the south side of the river Plate, fifteen leagues from its mouth. They are the remnant of the most numerous nation, inhabiting the Missouri when first known to the French. Their ancient principal village was situated in an extensive plain, on the northern bank of the Missouri, just below the mouth of Grand river. Frequent wars with the Saukees and Renars, and repeated attacks of the small pox, have reduced them to about eighty warriors, and a state of dependance on the Ottoes. They are about three hundred souls. They have a just claim to an extensive and fertile country, and yet reside in the same village with the Ottoes, and accompany them in their hunting excursions.

The Ottoes, with whom the Missouries reside, were descendants from that nation, but now view them as their inferiors, and sometimes treat them with abuse. They have about one hundred and twenty warriors, and five hundred souls; claim no exclusive possession, and hunt on the Saline and Nimmehaw rivers, and the plains which are westward of them. Their hunting and cultivating the ground is similar to that of the Kanzas and Osage. They raise corn, beans, squashes, pumpkins, and tobacco. These two nations are at war with the Great and Little Osage, Mahas, Poncars, Sioux, Kanzas, and Loups; and at peace with the Panis proper, Saukees, and Ranars.

The Panis proper, reside on the same river, fifteen leagues further up, on the south side. Their number of warriors is four hundred, and about sixteen hundred people. Their hunting ground extends over fertile, well watered plains, interspersed with groves of timber, especially along the water courses, and abounding with game. They are friendly and hospitable to white people; pay great respect to traders, with whom they are punctual in the payment of their debts. They cultivate corn, beans, melons, pumpkins, and tobacco. They are at war with the Great and Little Osage, Panis pique, Kanzas, La Play, Sioux, and Ricaras; and at peace with the Loups, Mahas, Poncars, Ottoes, and Ayauwais.

The Panis republican, or Big Paunch, is a band which has separated from the Panis proper, and established a village on a branch of the Kanzas river; but being harassed by their troublesome neighbours, the Kanzas, they have united themselves again with the Panis proper. They have three hundred warriors, and fourteen hundred souls.

Another branch of the Panis proper, is the Panis Loups, or Wolves. They live on Wolf river, which enters into the river Plate. They hunt on Wolf river above their village, and on the river Plate, between Wolf and the river Corn de Cerf, or Elkhorn. They are rarely visited by traders, and carry their firs and peltry to the village of Panis proper. They cultivate corn, beans, and other vegetables. They have two hundred and eighty warriors, and are at war with all other nations near their excursions, except the Panis proper and Panis republican or Big Paunch. They consist of about one thousand people.

The Mahas was a powerful nation until lately, residing on the west bank of the Missouri, two hundred and thirty miles above the mouth of the Plate river. They could boast seven hundred warriors, were warlike, and a terror to their neighbours. But in the autumn of 1802, they were visited by the small pox, which made such ravages among them, as to reduce their warriors to less than three hundred, and to about six hundred souls. This distressing calamity induced them to burn their village and become a wandering people. They were then deserted by traders ; and a deficiency of arms and ammunitions, invited aggression from their neighbours, which further reduced them to one hundred and fifty warriors. They rove principally on the head waters of Wolf river, and on the river Quicurre, or Rapid river. This country is high, level, and open, well watered, and a good soil. They are good hunters, and well disposed towards the whites. They were lately attacked by the Tetons Bois Brule, who killed and took about sixty of them.

Poncars are the remnant of a nation, once respectable for its numbers. Their former residence was on a branch of the Red river, of Lake Winnipie; but being oppressed by the Sioux, they removed to the southward, and took up their residence on Poncar river, west of the Missouri, where they built and fortified a village, and remained some years. At length their implacable enemy, the Sioux, pursued them; reduced them to about fifty warriors, and two hundred people ; and compelled them to join and reside with the Mahas, whose language they speak.

The Ricaras are the remains of ten large tribes of the Panis, who have been reduced by the small pox and the Sioux, to about five hundred warriors, and two thousand souls, They live in fortified villages, claim no land, except that on which their villages stand, and the fields they improve; and hunt immediately in their own neighbourhood. The country in every direction around them, for several hundred miles, is entirely bare of timber, except on the water courses and steep declivities of hills, where it is sheltered from the ravages of fire. The remains of the ancient villages of these people are to be seen on many parts of the Missouri, from the mouth of the Tetone river, to the Mandans. The rapacious Sioux Tetons, rob them of their horses, plunder their gardens and fields, and sometimes murder them without opposition, claim the country around them, although they are the oldest inhabitants, and treat them as merely tenants at will. Still they maintain a partial trade with their oppressors, the Tetons, to whom they barter horses, corn, beans, and a species of tobacco which they cultivate, and receive in return guns, ammunition, kettles, axes, and other articles, brought from the river Saint Peters. The Ricaras obtain these horses and mules from their western neighbours, who frequently visit them for the purpose of traffic.

The Mandans, consisting of three hundred and fifty warriors, and twelve hundred and fifty inhabitants, are the most friendly, and well disposed Indians who live on the Missouri. They are brave, humane, and hospitable. Several years ago they lived in six villages, about forty miles below their present towns. From repeated visitations of the small pox, and the frequent attacks of the Sioux, they have been reduced to their present number. They live in fortified villages; claim no particular tract of country; hunt only in their own neighbourhood; raise corn, beans, melons, squashes, pumpkins, and tobacco. They barter these articles, and horses and mules, with their neighbours, the Assinniboins, for guns, ammunition, axes, kettles, and many other articles, which are purchased of the Canadian traders, on the Assinniboin river. The traders themselves frequently bring their merchandise to them. The Mandans, again, exchange the articles thus obtained, for horses, leather tents, furs, and peltry, with the Crow Indians, and many other nations, who visit them for the purpose of traffic. The trade carried on, at these villages, gives them some resemblance of mercantile towns. They reside on both sides of the Missouri, about sixteen hundred miles from its mouth.

The Ah-wah-ha-wa, or Gens de Soulier, is a small nation, very little different from the Mandans, excepting that they carry on a constant and unjust warfare with the defenceless Snake Indians. They have fifty warriors, and two hundred inhabitants. Their village is only three miles above the Mandans, on the south side of the Missouri. They claim to have been a part of the Crow Indians, whom they still acknowledge as relation, but have resided on the Missouri, as long back as their tradition extends.

The Minetares, or Gross Ventres, is a large nation, consisting of six hundred warriors, and two thousand five hundred souls. They claim no particular country, nor assign themselves any limits; their tradition is that they have always resided in their present villages. Their customs, manners, and dispositions, are similar to the Mandans. Their villages are on both sides of Knife river, near the Missouri, five miles above the Mandans. On account of the scarcity of wood, they leave their villages in the cold season, and reside in large bands, in camps, on different parts of the Missouri, as high up as Yellow Stone river, and west of their villages, about Turtle mountain. These people have suffered by the small pox, but have been able to resist the attacks of the Sioux.

The Ayauwais nation, reside forty leagues up the river Demoin, and consist of two hundred warriors, and about eight hundred souls. They are descendants from the ancient Missouri, and claim the country west of them to the Missouri, and to the boundary of the Saukees and Foxes; are a turbulent savage people, who frequently abuse their traders, and commit depredations on those who are ascending and descending the Missouri.

Saukees and Ranars or Foxes, are two nations so nearly consolidated into one, that they may be considered as the same people. They speak the same language, and live near together, on the west side of the Mississippi, one hundred and forty leagues above Saint Louis. Formerly they lived on the east side of the Mississippi, and still claim the land between the Ouiseonsin and Illinois rivers. They frequently hunt west of them, towards the Missouri, but consider both sides of the Mississippi their hunting ground. The Saukees have about five hundred warriors, and two thousand souls; the Foxes three hundred warriors, and twelve hundred souls. They raise large quantities of corn, beans, and melons. They are extremely friendly to the whites, but implacable enemies to those Indians with whom they are at war.

The Sioux is a large nation, but divided into many independent bands. They retain the common appellation of Sioux, but each band has its appropriate name. The number of warriors is two thousand five hundred and ninety, and seven thousand six hundred and ten souls. They are roving bands, without any fixed habitations for any considerable time, and are generally at war with most of the other Indian nations. They claim, as their hunting ground, a very extensive country, on the waters of the Missouri and Mississippi. The following are the principal bands.

Wahpatone band rove on the northwest side of Saint Peters, to the mouth of Chippeway river, and on the head waters of the Mississippi, including the Crow-wing river. Their lands are fertile and generally well timbered. They are only stationary at their village, while the traders are with them, which is commonly from October, to March; treat them with respect, and seldom attempt to rob them.

Mindawawarcarton band extend their hunting ground from the mouth of the Saint Peters, to the Crow-wing river, on both sides of the Mississippi. They live in tents of dressed leather, which they transport by means of horses and dogs, and ramble from place to place during the greater part of the year; and yet are the only band of the Sioux, who cultivate corn, beans, and other vegetables. Their land is level, fertile, and well watered. To their own traders they are friendly, but inveterate to those who carry merchandise to their enemies, the Chippeways.

Wahpacoota band rove in the country west of Saint Peters, from a place called *Hardwood* to the mouth of the Yellow Medicine river: never stationary only when their traders are with them, which is not at any fixed time; a great portion of their country is open plains, and tolerably fertile. They barter the articles they receive from the traders, with the Yanktons and Tetons, who live west of them, for horses, robes, and leather tents or lodges.

Sissatone band hunt on Saint Peters and upper portions of Red river of Lake Winnipie, which is a level, plain, fertile country, free of stones, and intersected with small lakes. It abounds with fur animals, the beaver, otter, and marten, which enables them to purchase more merchandise, in proportion to their number, than their neighbours. An Indian fair is attended in the month of May, at a place agreed upon, on the waters of James river, where this band repair and meet the Tetons, Yanktons of the North, and Ahnah. Here a considerable traffic is carried on, and merchandise exchanged for horses and other articles. These people are devoted to the interests of their traders.

Yanktons of the North inhabit a country which is almost one entire plain, destitute of wood, but a good soil and well watered.

Yanktons Ahnah are considered the best disposed Sioux, who rove on the banks of the Missouri; but they will suffer no trader to ascend the river if they can prevent it: they arrest the progress of all they meet with, and generally compel them to sell their merchandise at a price very nearly what they themselves fix upon it; but they do not often commit any other acts of violence on the whites. Their country is very fertile, consisting of wood land and prairie.

Tetons Bois Brule, Tetons Okandandas, Tetons Minnakineazzo, and Tetons Sahone are four bands which rove over a country, almost entirely level, where a tree is scarcely to be seen, unless it be by water courses, or steep declivities of a small number of hills. It is from this country that the Missouri derives most of its colouring matter; the earth is strongly impregnated with glauber salts, allum, copperas, and sulphur, and when saturated with water, large bodies of the hills are precipitated into the river. On this account the waters of the Missouri have a purgative effect on those who are not accustomed to use them. These four bands are the pirates of the Missouri, and considered the vilest miscreants of the savage race. They receive their regular supply of merchandise from the river Saint Peters, and treat the traders on the Missouri with the utmost contempt, whom they never fail to plunder, when it is in their power. Supplication, or submission renders them the more rapacious. They say, the worse they treat the traders, the more merchandise they will bring them, and will dispose of their articles on the better terms.

The Chyennes, la Chien Indians are the remnant of a nation once respectable for their numbers; formerly resided on a branch of Red river of Lake Winnipie, which still is called la Chieon, or Dog river. Oppressed by the Sioux, they removed to the west side of the Missouri, about fifteen miles below the mouth of Warricunne creek, where they built and fortified a village, but being pursued by their ancient enemies, the Sioux, they fled to the Black Hills, about the head of Chien river, where they wander in quest of the buffaloe, having no fixed residence. Their number of warriors is computed to be about three hundred, and about twelve hundred souls. They do not cultivate, but bring to market buffaloe robes of the best quality, and are well disposed towards the whites.

The We-te-pa-ha-to or Wetepahatoes are a wandering nation, live on the Paduca fork of the river Plate, in an open country; and raise a great number of horses, which they barter to the Ricaras, Mandans and other nations, for articles of European Manufactures. Including the Kiawas who often live with them, they have about two hundred warriors, and seven hundred souls. They are a well disposed people, are at peace with all their wandering neighbours, to the west, and particularly with the Ricaras, Mandans, Minetares, and Ahwahhaways, whom they occasionally visit for the purpose of traffic, but have a defensive war with the Sioux.

The Kiawas do not materially differ from the Wetepahatoes, who live near, and often with them, in perfect friendship.

The Kenenavish, or Gens de Vache, reside on the heads of the Paduca's forks of the River Plate, and on the forks of the Chien river. They rove in an open country, like that of the Wetepahatoes, and carry on the same traffic. Their number is about four hundred warriors, and fifteen hundred souls.

The Staetan, or Kites, reside on the head waters of the Chien river, and frequently with the Kenenavish; and very nearly resemble them in all respects. They consist of about one hundred warriors, and four hundred people.

The Kata is a small nation, who have only about seventy-five warriors, and three hundred souls. They live between the head waters of the north and south forks of the River Chien.

The Nemausin, or allebome, are a small people, having about fifty warriors, and two hundred souls, and are on the head waters of north fork of Chien river. The principal difference between this nation and the Wetepahatoes, Kiawas, Staetan, and Kataha is, that they never visit the Ricaras, but carry on defensive war with them and the Sioux.

The Dotame is a still smaller nation, having only thirty warriors, and about one hundred and twenty people, inhabiting the heads of the river Chien. They wander over an open country; raise great numbers of horses and mules; are a friendly, well disposed people.

The Castahana is a larger nation, who live between the sources of the Padoca's forks of the rivers Plate and Yellow Stone. They have thirteen hundred warriors, and five thousand souls. Like the Dotame, rove in an open country, and raise great numbers of horses and mules; are friendly and peaceable, but have a defensive war with the Sioux and Assinniboins.

The Kee-hat-sa, or Crow Indians, or Gens-des Corbeau is large, having nine hundred warriors, and three thousand five hundred people. They live on each side of the river Yellow Stone, about the mouth of Big-horn river. Their country is said to be fertile, well watered, and in most parts well timbered. These people are divided into four bands, called by themselves, Ahah-ar-ro-pir-no-pah, Noo-ta, Pa-rees-car, and E-hart-sar. They annually visit the Mandans, Minetares, and Ahwahaways, to whom they barter horses, mules, leather lodges, and many articles of Indian apparel, for which they receive guns, ammunition, axes, kettles, awls, and other European manufactures. When they return to their country, they are, in turn, visited by the Paunch and Snake Indians, to whom they barter most of the articles they have obtained from the nations on the Missouri, for horses and mules, of which those nations have a greater abundance than themselves. They also obtain of the Snake Indians, bridle bits, blankets and some other articles, which those Indians purchase of the Spaniards.

The Al-la-ka-we-ah, or Paunch Indians, or Gens de Panse, reside on each side of the Yellow Stone river, near the Rocky Mountains, and heads of the Big-horn river. They have eight hundred warriors, and two thousand three hundred souls. These are said to be a peaceable, well disposed nation. Their country is variegated, consisting of mountains, vallies, plains, and wood lands, irregularly interspersed. These people, as well as the Crow Indians, inhabit a country, which produces an abundance of the most valuable furred animals. They are rovers, and have no idea of exclusive right to the soil.

The Assinniboin nation consists of three bands, who, like the bands of the Sioux, are entirely independent, one of the other; they claim a national affinity, and never go to war with each other. They are the descendants of the Sioux, and partake of their turbulent and faithless disposition; frequently plundering, and sometimes murdering their own traders. The name by which this nation is generally known, was borrowed from the Chippeways, who call them *Assinniboin*, which signifies *Stone Sioux*, and are sometimes called Stone Indians.

Manetopa band, or Gens des Canoe, live on Mouse river, between the Assinniboin and the Missouri. They have two hundred warriors, and seven hundred and fifty souls. They do not cultivate; but dispose of buffaloe robes, tallow, dried and pounded mint, and grease, skins of the large and small fox, small and large wolves, antelopes, or cabree, and elk in great abundance; some brown, white, and grizzly bear, deer and lynx.

Oseegah band, or Gens des Tee, consist of two hundred and fifty warriors, and eight hundred and fifty people; reside about the mouth of the Little Missouri, and on the Assinniboin, at the mouth of Lapelle river. These people do nothing at cultivation, although the country in which they rove is tolerably fertile, open, and free of stone. They traffic in buffaloe meat, dried and pounded, and grease in bladders : the skins of wolves, a few beaver and buffaloe robes.

Mahtopanato band, or Gens de Grand Diable, rove on the Missouri, about the mouth of the White Earth river, and on the head of Assinniboin, at the mouth of Capelle river. Their number of warriors is about four hundred and fifty, and sixteen hundred people. Their traffic is nearly the same with the other bands.

The Chippeways, or Ojibaway are divided into three principal bands, which are distinguished by

Chippeways of *Leach lake*, who reside on an island in a small lake, called Leach lake, formed by the Mississippi river. They claim the country on both sides the Mississippi, from the mouth of the Crow-wing river to its source, and extending west of the Mississippi, to the land claimed by the Sioux, with whom they still contend for dominion; and the country east of the Mississippi, as far as Lake Superior, including the waters of the River Saint Louis. They consist of four hundred warriors, and sixteen hundred souls. They do not cultivate the land, but live principally on the wild rice, which they procure in great abundance on the borders of Leach lake, and the banks of the Mississippi. They trade with beaver, otter, black bear, rackoon, marten, mink, fisher and deer skins. Their numbers have been reduced by wars and the small pox.

12*

Chippeways of *Red lake* consist of about two hundred warriors, and seven hundred people, they live on the head of the Mississippi, and about Red lake. They hunt the same animals as the preceding band, and make and sell bark canoes.

Chippeways of *Pembena river* reside on the Red river, of Lake Winnipie, and about the mouth of Pembena river. The number of this band is about one hundred warriors, and three hundred and fifty souls. They hunt principally beaver, and kill some wolverine and lynx, live by hunting, and do not claim any particular extent of ground. The Chippeways are well disposed towards the whites, but excessively fond of spiritous liquors.

Algonquins consisting of two bands;

Algonquins of *Rainy lake* are computed to have one hundred warriors, and three hundred souls. They live about Rainy lake. Rainy lake river and the Lake of the Woods. They live very much in detached small parties; are well disposed towards the whites, and deal principally in birch canoes.

Algonquins of the *Portage de Prairie* have two hundred warriors, and about six hundred people. They are emigrants from the Lake of the Woods, and live in a low, flat country, on Red river, and the Assinniboins, where there is an abundance of game.

The Christenoes, or Knistenaus, or Cree Indians, are a wandering nation, on the heads of

Assinniboin, and towards the Saskashawan river; do not cultivate, but take and traffic in beaver, otter, lynx, wolverine, mink, marten, wolf, small fox or kitts, dressed elk, and moose deer skins. They have three hundred warriors, and one thousand souls. Their language differs but little from the Chippeways, and have probably an affinity to that nation. These people sometimes visit Fort Dauphin mountains; are not esteemed good beaver hunters; are well disposed to the whites, and treat their traders with respect.

The A-lan-sar, or Fall Indians, are supposed to have six hundred and sixty warriors, and two thousand five hundred people; reside on the south fork of the Saskashawan river, and streams supposed to be branches of the Missouri. They trade with the northwest company; the country over which they rove is not much known.

The Cattanahaws is a wandering nation, near the Fall Indians; their number is not assertained.

The Tut-see-was or Flat-head Indians live on the west side of the Rocky mountains, on waters supposed to run into the Columbia river. The most that is known of the Flat-heads, is from the Minetares, or Grossventres, who are at war with them, and often take prisoners. They say that this nation resides in one village on the west side of a large and rapid river, which runs from south to north, at the foot of Rocky mountains. Their number is not ascertained ; are a timid, inoffensive people, and possess an abundance of horses.

The Aliatans are divided into three bands; of which there are several subdivisions.

Aliatans, So-so-na, *Snake Indians*, or Gens des Serpent, are a very numerous, well disposed people, inhabiting the Rocky mountains on the head of the Missouri, Yellow Stone, and Plate rivers. This band is divided into three large tribes, who wander at a considerable distance from each other; and are called by themselves, So-so-na, So-so-bu-bar, and I-a-kar. A part of these Indians live at, and near the falls of the Missouri. They raise a number of horses and mules, and often steal them from the nations who live east of them. These they sell to the Crow Indians ; they also carry on a partial trade with Spaniards, from whom they receive many articles of clothing and ironmongery, but the Spaniards never supply them with warlike instruments. Their numbers are not known, but are numerous.

Aliatans of *the West*, A-li-a-ta, live among the Rocky mountains, and on the plains at the heads of the Plate and Arkansas rivers. They have more intercourse with the Spaniards of New Mexico, than the Snake Indians, and receive many articles of merchandise from them ; but the Spaniards take the precaution not to furnish them with arms, and yet, in their unarmed state, they frequently commit hostilities. They are said to be very numerous, but the number unknown; are a warlike people, though badly armed. They have large numbers of horses, asses, and mules, and considerable quantities of buffaloe, deer, elk, black bear, antelope, and large horses, as well as the skins of many animals of the fur kind.

Aliatans, *La Plays*, principally inhabit the rich plains, from the head of the Arkansas, embracing the heads of Red river, and extending to the mountains on the borders of New Mexico. They possess no fire arms, but are warlike and brave; for the Spaniards fear these people, and take care not to furnish them with the implements of war. Their country abounds with wild horses, and raise immense numbers of horses, asses, and mules themselves. The number of these people is great, but not ascertained. These, as well as all the other Aliatans, are wandering people, and have no fixed place of residence.

The Caddo, or Caddoques, residing on Red river, have already been mentioned. These people, some years ago, left their ancient villages, called Caddo old towns, and settled on another part of Red river, nearer to Natchitoches, where they were visited with sickness, particularly the small pox and measles, by which nearly one half of them died. They had the small pox in the winter season, and as soon as the eruption appeared, they plunged into the water, which often proved fatal, in a few hours. The number of warriors of the ancient Caddo is reduced to about one hundred, who are viewed as a distinguished military order of men; they have many old men and strangers, who live amongst them, amounting to nearly an equal number with the Caddos. This nation has great influence over the Yattassees, Nandakoes, Nabadaches, Inies, Nagogdoches, Keychies, Adaize, and Natchitoches, who all speak the Caddo language, look up to them as their fathers, intermarry among them, and join them in all their wars. They cultivate corn, beans, pumpkins, melons, and tobacco.

The Yattasees live on Bayau Pierre or Stony creek, which falls into Red river fifty miles above Natchitoches. Their village is in a large prairie fifty miles above Natchitoches, and about midway to the Caddos. They are surrounded by a settlement of French families; but the Spanish government exercises jurisdiction over this settlement, where they keep a guard of a non-commissioned officer, and eight soldiers. The French formerly had a station and factory here, and another on the Sabine, about one hundred northwest of this settlement. Of the ancient Yattassees, there are about eight men remaining, and twenty-five women, besides children; but a number of men of other nations have intermarried, and live with them. They live on rich land; raise plenty of corn, beans, tobacco, and other vegetables: have horses, cattle, hogs, and poultry.

The Nandakoes live on the Sabine river, sixty or seventy miles to the westward, near where the

French formerly had a station and factory. A few years ago they suffered very much by the small pox, and are reduced to about forty men. They consider themselves the same as the Caddos, with whom they intermarry; visit one another in the greatest harmony; have the same manners, customs and attachments.

The Adaize live about forty miles from Natchitoches, on a lake called Lac Macdon, which communicates with the division of Red river, that passes by Bayau Pierre. They live where their ancestors have lived, time immemorial; the nearest nation to the old Spanish fort, or Mission Adaize; only twenty men of them remain, but there are more women. Their language differs from all other, and is said to be so difficult to speak or understand, that no nation can speak ten words of it; but they all speak Caddo, and most of them French; to whom they were always attached, and joined them against the Natchez Indians, after the massacre of Natchez, in 1728. While the Spaniards occupied Adaize, some priests attempted to proselyte them to the Roman Catholic religion, but without the smallest success.

The Aliche, pronounced Eyeish, reside near Nacogdoches. They were some years ago a considerable nation, and lived on a bayau of the same name, about twelve miles west of the Sabine river, but the small pox destroyed the most of them. The nation is now almost extinct, having only twenty-five souls remaining. Their native language is spoken by no other nation, but they speak and understand Caddo, with whom they are in friendship.

The Keyes, or Keychies, live on the east band of Trinity river, a small distance above where the road crosses from Natchitoches to Saint Antoine. They consist of only sixty men; have their peculiar language, but speak Caddo; intermarry with them, and live in great harmony. They plant corn and other vegetables.

The Inies, or Tachies, live about twenty-five miles west of Natchitoches, on a small river, which is a branch of the Sabine. This nation, like all their neighbours, is diminished, having only about eighty men; speak the Caddo language, and live in amity with them. They possess rich land and raise corn to sell.

The Nabedaches reside about fifteen miles above them, on the same river; consist of about the same number of men; speak the same language; improve the best of land; raise corn in plenty; and have the same customs and habits.

The Bedies are on the Trinity river, about sixty miles southward of Nacogdoches. They have about one hundred men, who are good hunters of deer, which are very large and plenty about them. Their language differs from all others, but speak Caddo; are a peaceable, quiet people; and have an excellent character for their honesty and punctuality. They plant and raise large crops of corn.

The Accokesaws live in a rich and beautiful country, over which they rove, often changing their place of residence; but their ancient town, and where they principally reside, is on the west side of Colerado or Rio Rouge. The deer they kill are said to be remarkably large and fat, of which they have an abundance. Their number of men is about eighty; they have a language peculiar to themselves; but they converse much by dumb signs, which they can all readily understand.

The Mayes live on a large creek, called Saint Gabriel, on the bay of Saint Bernard, near the mouth of Guadaloupe river. They are at perpetual war with the Spaniards, but very friendly to the French. Their number of men are computed to be two hundred. They have a language of their own, but speak the Attakapa, and likewise converse by signs.

The Carankouas, inhabit an island, or peninsula, in the bay of Saint Bernard. They are always at war with the Spaniards, and kill them whenever they find them; but kind to the French. They are said to be five hundred men strong; speak the Attakapa language, and are friendly to all other Indians.

On one side of this peninsula is a high bluff, or mountain of coal, which can be seen some distance at sea. It has been on fire for many years; affording a light by night, and a thick smoke by day, which has deceived and endangered vessels approaching the shoal waters on this coast. There is emitted from this burning coal, a gummy substance, which the Spaniards call *cheta;* it is thrown on the shore by the surf, and collected in considerable quantities; it has a strong aromatic smell, and not disagreeable to the taste. It is collected for the purpose of chewing, for which the Spaniards have a particular fondness.

The Cances are very numerous, consisting of a large number of different bands, occupying different parts of the country, from the bay of Saint Bernard, cross the river Grand, towards La Vera Cruz. They are unfriendly to the Spaniards, and kill them when they have opportunity; but are strongly attached to the French. They principally use the bow, and are good hunters. These people are very particular in their dress, differing from most of the other Indians. The dress of the men is straight leather leggins, which resemble pantaloons, and a leather hunting shirt, or frock. The women dress in a long, loose robe, which so entirely covers them, that nothing but their heads and feet are to be seen. No estimate can be made of the numbers of this nation. The Spaniards made slaves of these Indians, and sold numbers of them to the French at Natchitoches; but this practice was prohibited by the King of Spain, and those made slaves were emancipated;

after which some of the women who had been servants in good families, and taught spinning, sewing, and household work, married, and became respectable, well behaved women. Some of them are still living, and have brought up decent families of children. They have a peculiar language, and are understood by signs, in conversing with others. They are at peace with all nations except the Hietans.

The Tankaways or Tanks, claim no exclusive right to any tract of land; are always roving, and have no particular place of abode. They wander over the country watered by the Trinity, Braces, and Colerado, towards Saint a Fè. Their number of men are estimated at about two hundred; are one horde or tribe; dress like the Cances; are good hunters with the bow; and raise the best breed of horses. They are sometimes enimies, and at others, friends to the Spaniards. They plant nothing, but live on meat and wild fruit; are a strong athletic people, and excellent horse men.

The Tawakenoes, or Three Canes, reside on the west side of the Braces, and make their usual place of aboad, about two hundred miles west of Nacogdoches, towards Saint a Fè; but make their excursions as low down as the Great Prairies about the Turtle mountain. They are estimated at about two hundred men; are good hunters, principally with the bow, but have some guns. They speak the language of the Panis, and claim the same ancestors.

The Hietans or Comanches have neither towns nor villages, nor any fixed place of residence. They are divided into so many bands or tribes, that they have scarcely any knowledge of one another. No estimate of their numbers can be made. They never reside in the same place more than a few days, but constantly follow the buffaloe, which afford them their principal food. They carry their tents with them, which are made of neatly dressed skins, in the form of a cone; they are large enough for a family of ten or twelve persons; those of the chiefs are larger, and are some of them sufficient for fifty or sixty people. When they encamp, their tents are pitched in very exact order, so as to form regular streets and squares, which in a few minutes has the appearance of a handsome town, raised, as it were, by enchantment; and they are equally dexterous in striking their tents and preparing to march, when the signal is given. They allot two horses or mules to every tent, one to carry the tent, and the other the poles used in setting it up, which are neatly made of red cedar. They all travel on horse back. They never turn their horses loose to graze, but keep them tied with a long halter; and every two or three days they are obliged to move, to find grass for the support of their horses; for they have always a large number. They have fine horses, and are excellent horse men. Most of their horses are bred by themselves, and by handling them when very young they are remarkably docile and gentle. Sometimes wild horses are caught and tamed, which are every where amongst them in large droves. They hunt down the buffaloe on horse back, and kill them either with the bow, or a sharp wooden spear, which they carry in their hands. They are said, when they kill a buffaloe, to catch and drink the blood, while it is warm; they likewise eat the liver raw, before it is cold, and use the gall for sauce. They are, for savages, uncommonly neat and clean in their persons and dress. The women wear a long, loose robe, which reaches from the chin to the ground, with a fancy sash or girdle around the waist, all made of neatly dressed leather, on which they paint figures of different colours and significations. The dress of the men is close leather pantaloons, and a hunting frock, made of leather. They cultivate no vegetables, but they season their food with a small cayenne pepper, which grows spontaneously in the country, and some wild herbs. They also make use of wild fruits, particularly a bean, which grows in great plenty on a small tree, resembling a willow, called *masketo*. With these articles the women will cook their buffaloe beef in a manner highly grateful to the taste. They occupy alternately a vast extent of country from the Trinity, Braces, the head of Red river, and Arkansas, to the Missouri, River Grand, about Saint a

13*

Fè, and over the mountains, to the waters of the western ocean. They say, they have seen big peroques, with masts, which they describe by drawing a ship and the sails and rigging. Their language sounds different from that of any other nation, and none can either speak or understand it; but they have a language by signs, whch can be understood by all Indians; and which they use much in conversing among themselves. They are generally at war with the Spaniards, and often commit depredations on the inhabitants of Saint a Fé, and Saint Antoine; but have always been friendly to the French or Americans, who have been among them. They have a number of Spanish men and women among them; who are slaves, and who were made prisoners when they were young.

The following story is related by an elderly gentleman, living at Natchitoches, who formerly carried on a trade with this nation. A number of years ago, a party of these Indians passed over the River Grand, to Chewawa, the residence of the governor-general of what is called the five internal provinces; lay in ambush for an opportunity, and made a prisoner of the governor's daughter, a young lady, as she was going in her coach to mass, and brought her off. The governor sent a message to this gentleman, with a thousand dollars, for the purpose of recovering his daughter: he immediately dispatched a confidential trader, then in his employ, with the amount of the thousand dollars in merchandise, who repaired to the nation, and after he had found her, purchased her ransom; but to his great surprise, she refused to return with him to her father, and sent by him the following message: that the Indians had disfigured her face, by tattooing it according to their fancy and ideas of beauty, and a young man of them had taken her for his wife, by whom she believed herself pregnant; that she had become reconciled to her mode of life, and was well treated by her husband; and that she should be more unhappy by returning to her father, under these circumstances, than by remaining where she was. Which message was conveyed to her father, who rewarded the trader by a present of three hundred dollars more for his trouble and fidelity; and that, at the time of relating this account, his daughter was living with her Indian husband, in the nation, by whom she had had three children.

The Natchitoches nation formerly lived, where the town of Natchitoches is now situated, which took its name from them. About one hundred years ago, when the French began their settlement in this town, this nation had six hundred men. They became attached to French people, and have ever been their steady and faithful friends. After the massacre of the French inhabitants of Natchez, by the Natchez Indians, in 1728, those Indians fled from the French, after the French were reinforced, and came up Red river, and camped about six miles below the town of Natchitoches, near the river, by the side of a small lake of clear water, and erected a mound of earth, of considerable size, where it now remains. Monsieur Saint Dennie, a French Canadian, was then commandant at Natchitoches; the Indians called him the Big Foot, were fond of him, for he was a brave man. Saint Dennie, with a few French soldiers, and what militia he could muster, joined by the Natchitoches Indians, attacked the Natchez Indians in their camp, early in the morning; they defended themselves desperately for six hours, but were at length totally defeated, and what were not killed in battle, were drove into the lake, were the last of them perished, and the Natchez, as a nation, became extinct. This lake is now called Natchez lake. Since that time the Natchitoches nation have decreased, until their remains only twelve men, and nineteen women, who live in a village about twenty-five miles above the town, near a lake called by the French Lac de Muire. The small pox has been their great destroyer. Their original language is the same as the Yattassee, but speak Caddo and French. The French inhabitants highly respect this nation, and a number of decent families have a mixture of their blood in them. They still preserve their Indian dress, and habits; raise corn and the other vegetables common in their neighbourhood.

There are the remains of several more nations, who are become nearly extinct, inhabiting in different parts of this country, who are mostly emigrants from the eastern side of the Mississippi. The *Boluxas*, from Pensacola, live on Red river, at the mouth of Rigula de Bandieu, who are reduced to about thirty men. They are an honest, harmless, and friendly people. The *Appalaches* from West Florida, live above bayau Rapide, and consist of only fourteen men. The *Allibamis* came from West Florida, consist of seventy men, of whom thirty have settled near the Caddoques, and forty in Appelousa district. *Conchattas* are from West Florida, call their number one hundred and sixty men, and are settled on the River Sabine. Several families live in detached settlements, which they say will make their number two hundred men. *Pacanas* are also emigrants from West Florida, are a small tribe of about thirty men, and live on the Quelqueshoe river. *Attakapas*, a name which is said to mean man-eater, but no more applicable to this tribe, than that of any other Indians. Their number, including some Tunicas and Humas Indians, who have intermarried and live with them, is about eighty men. They are peaceable and friendly to every body, and are settled between Attakapa church and the Quelqueshoe river. The *Appelousa*, which means black head or black skull, have about forty men, are natives of the district called by their name, and live west of Appelousa church.

Tunicas do not exceed twenty-five men, and live at Avoyall. *Pascagolas* from West Florida, have only twenty-five men, and live in a small village on Red river. *Tenisaws* are emigrants from Tenesau river, which falls into the bay of Mobile, are reduced to twenty-five men, and live on bayau Beauf. *Chactoos* live on the same bayau; are aborigines of the country where they live, and are diminished to about thirty men. *Washas* are reduced to two men and three women, and live in French families. The *Chactaws* have two villages, one consisting of thirty, and the other of fifty men, in the district of Appelousa, besides rambling hunting parties, in different parts of the country. They are at war with the Caddoques, and not liked by either red or white people. The *Arkansas*, who claim three hundred miles on that river, but live in three villages, are supposed not to exceed three hundred men. They speak the Osage language, but are at war with that nation. They raise corn to sell, and are called an honest and friendly people.

These Indian nations reside, or rove in their hunting and trading excursions, within what has been conjectured to be the limits of Louisiana. In ascertaining their numbers, it was unavoidably necessary, in many instances, to depend on Indian information; but it is presumed that the number of warriors, which is generally given in even numbers, is not far from being correct; and calculating on the best data that could be obtained, the souls are probably estimated rather below, than above their real number.

In constructing the following table, for the purpose of giving a collected view of the number of each nation, and an aggregate of the whole of those nations which are so numerous, and so divided and subdivided into bands and parties, that their numbers could not be known by any information the Indians were able to give, are presumed to be, at least, equal to the Great and Little Osage nation, and their numbers are assumed; and those nations of whom only the number of men are ascertained, the number of souls are calculated in about the same proportion to the number of warriors, with those of the other nations.

Indian Nations.	Warriors.	Souls.
Great and Little Osage,	2000	8000
Kanzas,	300	1200
Missouris,	80	300
Ottoes,	120	500
Panis Proper,	400	1600
Panis Republican, or Big Paunch,	300	1400
Panis Loups, or Wolf Indians,	280	1000
Maha,	300	600
Pancars,	50	200
Ricaras,	500	2000
Mandans,	350	1250
Ahwahhawa,	50	200
Minetares, or Grossventres,	600	2500
Ayauwais,	200	800
Saukees,	500	2000
Renars, or Fox Indians,	300	1200
Sioux, (ten bands)	2590	7610
Chien, or Dog Indians,	300	1200
Wetepahatoes and Kiawas,	200	700
Kenenavish,	400	1500
Staetan, or Kites,	100	400
Kata,	75	300
Nemousin, or Allebome,	50	200
Dotame,	30	120
Castahana,	1300	5000
Keehatsa, or Crow Indians,	900	3500
Allakaweah, or Paunch Indians,	800	2300
Assinniboin consisting of three bands,	900	3100
Chippeways, three bands,	700	2650
Algonquins, two bands,	300	900
Christenoes, or Cree Indians,	300	1000
Alansar, or Fall Indians,	660	2500
Cattananaws, (supposed to be)	600	2000
Tutsee, or Flat Head,	300	900
Alitans, or Snake Indians, (supposed,)	2000	8000
Caddoques,	100	400
Yattasees,	8	57
Nandakoes,	40	160
Adaize,	20	85
Aliche,	5	25
Keyes,	60	240
Inies,	80	320

Indian Nations.	Warriors.	Souls.
Nabedaches,	80	320
Bedies,	100	400
Accokesaws,	80	320
Mayes,	200	800
Carankouas,	500	1200
Cances, (numerous supposed to be,)	2000	8000
Tankaways, or Tanks,	200	800
Tawakenoes, or Three Canes,	200	800
Hietans, (numerous supposed to be,)	2000	8000
Natchitoches,	12	65
Boluscas,	30	120
Appalaches,	14	56
Allibamis,	70	280
Conchattas,	200	800
Pacanas,	300	1200
Attakapas,	80	300
Appelousa,	40	160
Tunicas,	25	100
Pascagolas,	25	100
Tenisaws,	25	100
Chactoos,	30	120
Washas, men 2, women 3,	2	5
Chactaws,	80	320
Arkansas,	300	1200
	25,741	94,403

THE
JOURNAL
OF
Mr. CHARLES LE RAYE.

In the year 1801, I left Canada with an adventure of goods, to trade on the Missouri. I arrived at the French settlement on the Illinois, early in September, and concluded to ascend the Osage river, and to trade with the Osage nation. Here I procured two additional hands, which completed my complement of six men besides myself. As soon as my perioque was finised, we embarked. On the 21st of September, I entered the mouth of the Missouri, and as the waters were low, we ascended with ease.

On the 7th of October, entered the Osage river, and ascended seven miles, where we encamped to hunt, and procure meat. Nothing material occured until the 23d, when we had ascended within sixty miles of the Osage village, and had encamped for the night, at a small stream, on the east side of the river. After supper I ordered the men, who were in a tent on the shore, to keep a watch, as usual, and retired to the perioque to sleep. Just before day, I was awaked by the rushing of a number of Indians through the brush, and before I could disengage my self and my gun from the buffaloe robe, in which I was enwrapped, an Indian, followed by five or six more, rushed into the boat, and seizing my gun, dragged me on shore. As soon as they had bound me, I was hurried back into the boat, and seven Indians jumping in, they bushed the boat from the shore, and hurried down the river, as fast as they could paddle. I saw a large number on the bank around the tent. It was so dark I could not distinctly see my men, but heard the voice of one of them speaking to the Indians, in the Osage tongue. From this, I concluded they were Osage Indians.

The Indians in the boat proceeded with me down the river about twenty miles, and came to their encampment, kept by four lads, fourteen or fifteen years old. Here they unloaded the boat. I was anxious to know the fate of my men, and about noon was much relieved by seeing them brought in by the rest of the party. The number of Indians now, were forty-six men, and four lads. They immediately collected their horses, fourteen in number, and the goods were loaded on them. We were all bound with buffaloe cords over our arms, and, travelling up the branch, until about midnight, we encamped. When we lay down to sleep, we were secured between two Indians, one of which had the end of the cord with which we were bound, around his body. In the morning, after eating some dried meat, for which purpose our arms were loosened, we pursued a course, north or west, and leaving the creek, we crossed several ridges covered with grass, but entirely destitute of timber. About noon we crossed a small stream, a branch of the stream we had ascended, and encamped on it, at night. On the 25th of October, we travelled through a country somewhat broken, and destitute of timber, but game was very plenty, and two deer were shot. At night we encamped by an excellent spring. There being no wood, we kindled a fire with dry weeds, and broiled meet for our suppers.

On the 26th we set forward early, and continuing a west course, came to a stream of water which one of my men, who had been on the Missouri, said, was a branch of Mine river. The country became more level, with some small timber near the water. I now discovered that the Indians were not Osage, but a party of Sioux, of the Bois Bucil band. We encamped on the branch, and on rich land. On the 27th, we continued down the stream until we came to a small path, where the land was covered with high grass and weeds. We encamped at the mouth of the stream. On the 28th, we crossed the stream, and proceeded a west course to Mine river, and crossing the river, we encamped on the west side, on rich land, covered with large timber. Here we tarried part of the day to hunt, having no other provision than some corn, taken from the perioque. During the day the cords were taken from our arms. The guns and ammunition taken from the perioque were sufficient to furnish the Indians, so that most of them were well armed, and only a few of them made use of their bows.

On the 29th, we left Mine river, and continued a west course until we came to a large beaten path, which was the Kanzas war path to the Missouri. We continued in the path a few miles, and left it to the right. We encamped on a small run, with scarcely water sufficient to quench our thirst. Proceeding early on the 30th, we travelled through a level, rich country destitute of timber. At this time my feet, and the feet of some of my men, had become so sore as scarcely to be able to walk. Coming to a branch of the Kanzas river, we encamped. As soon as the camp was made, a keg of rum taken from the perioque was broached, and soon all the Indians, except the chief, four warriors and the four lads, were drunk. After a very noisy night, towards morning they fell a sleep. They had taken great care to secure us before they began to drink. In the hurry last evening to taste the rum, they had neglected to give us any thing to eat. This morning, (31st), our appetites were of course good, as we had not tasted any thing but water and a little spirit since the preceding morning. We therefore eat an hearty breakfast, and assisted in loading the

14*

horses. The Indians after they awoke were again for tasting the spirits, but this being opposed by the chief, and the horses being loaded, we proceeded. Continuing our course down a branch of the Kanzas, started a drove of buffaloe, consisting of two or three hundred. The Indians killed six, and then encamped on the branch. I expected the rum would have been broached, but their debauch the night before seemed to have satisfied them. Here they informed us, that in two days we should arrive at the camp where their women were.

November 1st, we continued down the branch. Snow fell some depth last night. Proceeded early on the 2d, and found the country somewhat hilly, but destitute of timber, except near the water. On the 3d, it rained, and we continued in the camp. Three men were sent forward to notify the band of our approach. Towards noon the weather cleared up, and we proceeded about six miles, and met the whole band, consisting of about two hundred men, women and children. As soon as the chief discovered the band, he set up the yell, and was answered by the band, which formed two lines, opening to the right and left, and we were led between them. Some of the children shewed a dispositon to insult us, but were prevented by the men. The whole proceeded to the encampments, where the tents were all standing in two rows, facing each other. Under different circumstances I should have been pleased with the appearance. But at this time my mind was occupied with anxiety about my fate, and that of my companions, expecting to be tomehawked or burned. On our arrival we were taken to the centre of the encampment, where the two chief tents were situated, and my self and companions put into the tents belonging to the chief who had taken us. The goods were unloaded and distributed among the Indians. While this was doing, a Frenchman came into the tent and spoke to me, which much revived my spirits. As soon as he had learned that we were all Frenchmen, he left us; but soon returned with the consoling news that we should be well treated. The chief soon after came in, ordered us unbound, and that some meat should be given us to eat. His squaws were now bringing in his share of the goods. The chief seated himself, and then the other chief and the warriors came in, and after lighting their pipes, entered into a long conversation, in the Sioux tongue, with the Fenchman. As soon as the conversation ended, my men were distributed among the warriors, and I was retained by the chief who took me. The name of the Frenchman, who resided with this people, was Pardo. He informed me no further injury was intended me, or my men. He also informed me that this was a party that went in pursuit of some Osage Indians, who, a short time before, had killed some of their band, and that their meeting with me was accidental; but suspecting me to be taking goods and arms to the Osage Indians, their enemies, they took me. In the evening the rum was again broached. Two kegs of high proof spirits had been taken from the perioque, which contained about twelve gallons each. I was directed not to leave the tent.

Early in the morning of the 4th, I went out and found all still. At the farther part of the encampment, where the liquor was drank, I saw the horrid effects of their last night's debauch. The wood, weeds, and almost every thing, was covered with blood. While I was viewing the scene, an Indian came to me, and bid me begone. I therefore immediately returned to the tent. Soon after Mr. Pardo came in and told me the Indians had been very drunk, and had fought with their knives. Three of them were badly wounded, and one very dangerously. I was permitted to take several small articles from the chief's share of the goods, among which were my papers, a razor and a lappo coat. These I procured through the influence of Mr. Pardo. He informed me that in a few days the band would go to the Ricarus village, where more of the band were. This camp in which we now were, was situated on a lage fork of the Kanzas, on the edge of a prairie. The tents were made of buffaloe skins dressed, and painted with a variety of rude figures, which at a distance made a handsome appearance. Each tent was set up in form of a cone, by means of a pole about twelve feet long, with the skins tied round it, at the top, and spread out at the bottom. The doors of the tents were made facing each other, before which they made a fire, and some times one in the tent. It was several days before the wounded Indians could be moved, and during our stay the Indians killed a deer, which is called the long tailed deer. It was larger than the red deer, of a darker colour, and with a white belly. Its horns are short, small and somewhat flat; its tail nearly eighteen inches long. They are said to be plenty in these plains.

The wounded Indians having so far recovered as to be able to be transported, on the 12th, we prepared for our departure, and removed a few miles. The Indians now treated me with a much greater degree of hospitality, than, from their former conduct, I had any reason to expect. On the 13th, we continued our course to the Kanzas river. This is a handsome stream, about twice as wide as the Osage, and flows through a rich country, but mostly destitute of timber, except on the water courses. We crossed it about forty miles from the mouth. The Kanzas nation of Indians reside near its head waters. On the 14th, continued a northwest course in a well beaten path, and the country somewhat hilly. The 15th, crossed a small stream of water running to the northwest, the land hilly, without timber. From this time to the 20th, very little difference in the appearance of the country. On the 20th, came to a branch of the river La

Plate. The land now became rich and level, with wood near the water. Here the Indians separated, and about one hundred and fifty directed their course towards the Missouri, with whom all my men were taken. Mr. Pardo, myself, the chief who took me, and the rest of the Indians, continued our course towards the Ricaras village.

On the 24th, came to the River La Plate. This is a rapid stream, not less than three forths of a mile in width. It comes from a great distance from towards the south. The Panis, Ottoes, Missouri and Wolf Indians, live on the waters of this river, and are all at war with the Sioux. On the 25th, we crossed the river with great difficulty and danger, owing to the running of the ice.

On the 26th, some of the squaws made themselves carriages, to transport their baggage, by lashing three or four bars to the ends of two slim poles, and yoking a dog to the poles. A dog, in this manner, will draw about seventy pounds. The snow was now about eight inches deep. We continued our course on the 27th, northwesterly. Here the country became more broken, ascending into ridges. There were a considerable number of elk, buffaloe, cabree or antelope, and deer, and very little timber to be seen on these ridges.

Nothing material occurred until the 2d day of December, when we came to the Missouri, and crossed it near the mouth of the Little Pioux. We continued our course on the north side of the Missouri, often near it, until we arrived at the lodges, on the Sioux river, which was on the 8th, where we prepared to spend the remainder of the winter. It was found that several of the Indians had got frozen. They were very slightly clothed, having nothing more than a buffaloe robe, or a deer, or cabree skin, thrown over their shoulders, with only leggins, their moccasons being worn out. The weather was now very severe, and the lodges illy calculated to shelter us from it. We covered and patched them up, as well as we could, with dry grass and willow branches. In the centre an opening was made, ten feet in length, and eighteen inches in width, for the purposes of letting out the smoke, and leting in the light. The doors were made close with buffaloe skins. During the night, the horses are sheltered under the same cover with the people, being only separated by a pole. They are fed in the night on willow and button wood branches, and in the day time are turned out to graze on whatever they can find to eat.

These Indians are the dirtiest creatures on earth. They bring their water for themselves and their horses, in the paunches of the deer and cabree, which are never cleansed more than what is done by constant use. Their meat is cooked in the most filthy manner. When they boil it, they continue the boiling until it can be eaten with a spoon, throwing in a handful of corn, if they have it, with a small quantity of bear's oil; but make use of no seasoning of any kind. When it is ready to eat, the whole company, with ten or fifteen dogs, gather round it, and each one strives to get his share. They have no set times for their meals, but it seems to depend on the calls of hunger, and a disposition to prepare the food.

An animal is found in these plains, called le prairie chein, or prairie dog. It is smaller than the grey fox, and formed much like the dog. Its ears are pointed and stand erect, and the whole head very much resembles the dog. Its tail is long, slim, and of a dun colour. It digs holes and burrows in a light, loamy soil, and in the same holes, a small speckled snake takes shelter, which the Indians call the dog's guard. The Indians have many superstitious notions respecting these dogs. The Ay-oo-wars, or Nespeirce nation have a tradition that the human race sprang from this dog and the beaver. All other nations hold them in great veneration. A kind of deer were frequently killed here, called mule deer. It is smaller and of a darker colour than the red deer, having large, branched horns. The ears are very large; the tail about five inches long, with short dark hair, and at the end, a tuft composed of long, black hair. A species of the badger, called prarow, inhabits these plains. Its head much resembles the dog; legs short and very thick in proportion to its body, armed with long, sharp claws, well adapted to digging. The size of the body somewhat exceeds the ground hog; hair of a dark brown colour, and tail, bushy, resembling that of the ground hog. It burrows and lodges in the ground.

In the latter part of winter we were much distressed for food. Hunting became bad, and game scarce. We had often nothing more than one poor dog boiled, to feed twenty for a day, and sometimes for a much longer space of time. The Indians are fond of dog's flesh, and at their feasts use no other kind of meat. During the winter, a few fish were taken in the river. These were principally the cat fish.

To my great satisfaction, on the 20th of March, 1802, we left this camp of filth and misery, where we had remained from the 8th of December, and proceeded towards the Ricaras, or Rus, as the traders call them. Some of the Indians had prepared themselves sleighs to ride in, which were made in the following manner. A slender frame was made of small sticks, woven together, about three feet in length, and the sides about eight inches high. Over this frame, deer or cabree skins were drawn tight, and came over the upper part, forward, about eighteen inches. It was then placed on two runners, made of bent poles, to the end of which was fastened two slim poles for shafts. The whole was secured together by buffaloe cords. Two dogs were then yoked to the shafts, one before the other, and the rider places himself in the sleigh, with his feet under the covered part. He then guides the foremost dog by a line fastened round his neck, and in this manner the dogs will draw him with great ease. We arrived on the banks of the Missouri, near the salt springs, on the 23d, and being unable to cross the river on account of the ice, which began to break up, we continued up the river to where the ice remained firm, and well secured by a sand bar in the middle of the river. Here we crossed, and proceeded up to White river, about twenty miles, where we arrived on the 27th, and encamped. On the 29th, we removed up the White river, sixteen miles, to hunt. The snow now began to disappear, and the plains were covered with game. Here no timber was to be seen except on the water courses, where a few willows, elm, and button wood grew, but the appearance of the soil was rich. A small party of Rus, joined us at this camp, and on the 6th of April, we crossed White river, which is about one hundred and fifty yards wide, and continued our journey towards the Rus village. On the 9th, we encamped on Tyler's creek ; and on the 12th, we arrived opposite Tuton river. Here we left the Missouri, and proceeded a west course to the River Chein, or Dog river. On this route we travelled through a broken country, destitute of wood, and badly watered. We arrived at the Chein river on the 14th, and immediately crossed it in buffaloe canoes. The river is nearly half a mile wide, and as the Indians informed me, flows through a plain, level country, for several hundreds of miles, mostly destitute of timber. On the head waters riside several tribes of Indians, with which the Sioux are at war. The most powerful of these tribes are the Chein, or Dog Indians. There are also the *Gens-di-rach*, or *Kananawesh*, the *Kites* and *Dotame*, besides bands of the *Mahas, Pancars*, and *Kataka*. We met with a camp of the Rus Indians, who were hunting, and continued here until the 18th, when they joined us, and we proceeded to the villages about sixty miles, travelling through a country destitute of timber, and interspersed with large hills. On the 22d, arrived at the lower village and joined several camps of Sioux and Dog Indians. The *Ricaras* or *Rus*, have three villages, situated on the south bank of the Missouri, in the great bend of the river. The lower village is on a large bottom, covered with cotton wood, and contains about fifty huts. These huts were built in a different manner, and were more comfortable habitations, than any Indian huts I had before seen. To build their huts, they cut four forked posts, which are set up fifteen feet high. Two of these posts stand eighteen inches apart, and two stand at the distance of ten feet from the other two posts, and ten feet from each other, on which two ridge poles are placed. Around these posts they erect sixteen forked posts more, six feet high, which are so placed as to form a circular figure, eighteen feet in diameter. On the front side two more posts, six feet long, are set up, ten feet from the building, and four feet apart. Short poles are then laid round on these sixteen forks, and on the forks of the two posts which project in front, to connect them with the building. Stakes are then placed in a reclining position, so as to lean against the poles which are placed on the six feet posts, and stand eight or nine inches apart. At the upper end of these stakes, poles are fastened, so that the other end rests upon the ridge poles. When the frame is thus completed, the whole is covered with willow and cotton wood branches, except an opening between the ridge poles, for the smoke to pass, and the space in the front of the projection, which is left for a door way. Over the branches is laid a covering of long grass, and over the grass, a coat of clay mortar.

These huts are placed with great regularity, in two straight rows. The doors in each row front those in the opposite row, so that the huts stand facing each other, with a space of twelve feet between the doors. The town is picketed with pickets, twelve feet high, and set very close, to prevent firing between them. There is one gate way, which is shut at night.

These people are much more cleanly in their persons, dress, and food, than the Sioux. They are also of a lighter complexion, which is of a bright copper colour, with aquiline noses and black, lively eyes. The women have high cheek bones, oval faces, and regular features. Both men and women are of a social, sprightly make. The men are tall and well formed, and the women, though smaller, are equally well shaped, and rather handsome, than otherwise. Their dress consists of a shift made of dressed deer skins, and reaches from the chin, below the knee, to the middle of the leg, with short sleeves. It is secured round the waist by a belt of wampum. They wear moccasons and leggins, and in the winter a buffaloe robe, thrown over their shoulders. The men wear a wide strip of leather, about three feet long, which they draw between their legs, and fasten it around the middle by a belt. They have long leggins and moccasons, and a buffaloe robe over their shoulders.

These Indians raise corn, beans, melons, pumpkins and tobacco. Their tobacco differs from that which is raised by white people. It has a smaller stalk, that grows about eighteen inches high, with long, narrow leaves, and is only used for smoking. The Indians never chew, nor snuff tobacco. They carry on, at these villages, a considerable commerce with these productions; having much more than they want for their own consumption. It is a barter trade with neighbouring nations, who never cultivate the ground, for such articles of European goods, as they have procured at the British establishments, at the falls of Saint Anthony, or from traders; and also for horses, mules, dried meat, and other articles. Their principal customers are the Sioux, the Chein Indians, *Watapahatoes*, *Gens-dis-vatch*, *Kites*, and *Dotame*, the most of whom, except the Sioux, reside on the river Chein. This nation was once very numerous, and consisted of ten tribes of the *Panis*, who reside on the river La Plate, and whose tongue they speak in somewhat of different accent. They have now not much over five hundred warriors; having been reduced from five thousand warriors, to their present number, in less than thirty years, by the small pox and attacks of their enemies; particularly by the Sioux, who have got them so far under subjection, that they dare not offend them, and are frequently robbed, plundered, and even murdered, without daring to resent it. This information was given me by an old chief of the lower villages.

Above the Sioux river, and between that and the River Sacque, is a small hill, destitute of timber, which the natives say is inhabited by spirits, in shape of human beings, of a very diminutive size, not being, according to their description, more than six or eight inches high. Respecting these bodily spirits they have a number of ridiculous fancies. An old chief told me, with great gravity, that the occasion of their coming and living on this hill, was, because the Indians, a great many winters ago, were so wicked and foolish, as to strive to kill all the animals made for their use. The Great Spirit saw them from above, and was so angry with them that he sent these little beings, which the Indians call Wakons, to drive all the animals out of the country, which they did, and many of the Indians starved for want of food. But after much entreaty and many sacrifices, the anger of the Great Spirit was appeased, and he permitted the animals to return; but directed the Wakons to reside on this hill, to watch the conduct of the Indians, and should they again be so wicked, they are to drive all the animals off, never to return. This impression has had an excellent effect on the natives, as it prevents causeless waste of what is so necessary for their subsistence. They pretend often to see these little beings on, and about the hill, as they are passing, but no consideration would induce an Indian to set his foot on this holy ground.

The lower village, on the 20th of May, held their great feast. Two days previous notice was given by their principal chiefs. There being a number of camps of different tribes, they were all invited to join, and in the morning of the festival, were dressed out in their best attire, and made no indifferent appearance. Their faces were daubed with a variety of paints. Their ears, noses and hair, were full of silver rings, and of silver and glass trinkets; with silver breast plates; and a multitude of beads, hanging round their necks. Their hair was also filled with the feathers of the eagle, and other large birds. Bandayes full of brooches were tied round their foreheads. Their clothes neatly worked with porcupine quills and beads, and large wampum belts around the middle. Their moccasons and leggins strung with bits of brass and beads, worked full of porcupine quills and horse hair dyed red. In this finical, gaudy dress, they all assembled in a place prepared for the purpose, near the village, in the fore part of the day. The men only partake of the feast, but the women are distant spectators; for they are never suffered to eat with the men, neither at feasts, nor in their own families, when strangers are present. This, however, does not prevent them from decorating themselves for the occasion. After all had assembled, the head chief of the village addressed the company in an impressive speech, in which he informed them, that it had been a practice, time immemorial, to celebrate the return of the spring, by a feast to the Great Spirit. He recommended to them peaceable and friendly behaviour, and told them, that as the Great Spirit had given them an unclouded sky, he was well pleased with their intention, and that each one should be careful not to offend him by improper conduct. After the address, the company were seated, and the head chief opened his medicine bag, from which he drew the sacred stem or pipe. This he placed on the forked sticks set in the ground before him for the purpose. Fire was then brought, and he lighted the pipe, and blowed the smoke to the east, south, west, and north; after which he handed the pipe to the chief next to him, on the right, who smoked two or three whiffs and passed it to the next, and so on, until it had gone round the company.

The provisions were now brought forward, composed entirely of dog's flesh, and placed before the great chief, and each one sent his dish to him, in turn; for before they came, every one took care to provide a dish for himself. Some of the youth attended as waiters to the company. The greatest order and regularity was observed during the feast. Each one considered himself obliged to eat all that was sent him; but at such feasts it is seldom more than they can devour in a few minutes. As soon as the feast was ended, fire was brought, and the whole commenced smoking, which was continued for about an hour. The smoking then ceased and the dance commenced. Their music consisted of beating on buffaloe skins, shaking dried prarow and marten skins, tied up, in a form to contain small stones, and beating on a kind of drum, made by stretching a skin, dressed like parchment, over the end of a hollow log about four feet long, which is joined with the singing of the company. Their songs are a rehearsal of the exploits of themselves and their ancestors, and is accompanied with a variety of antic gestures. In all their movements they keep exact time; dance in a circle around a fire, never taking hold of hands, nor touching one another, unless by accident. The dance continued until near morning. When the dance was closed, all retired to their respective quarters, perfectly quiet and peaceable. Although the company consisted of not less than a thousand people, of different nations, and some of whom were mortal enemies to others, there was not the least confusion heard during the day or night.

The Indians are extravagantly fond of gambling, and spend most of their leisure hours in it. The game they appear most attached to is played with eight bones, of the size of a man's finger, of an oval form, three fourths of an inch long, with four square sides, two of which are coloured black and red. They are placed on wooden trenchers, or oval platters. From this dish the bones are tossed into the air, and then caught in the dish. They win or lose according to the number of a certain colour, previously agreed upon, being uppermost, until the game is finished, which is always forty-five. Two bands or parties will play at this game, the loser rising and letting one of his party take his place, until the whole band has had a part in the game. They often play for all the property they possess, and after losing that, set up their wives and children, for they are considered the men's property, as much as their arms, or any thing they possess. Another game is played by means of small sticks, five inches long, of the size of a goose quill, neatly polished and marked with red and black lines. Forty of these sticks are divided between the two persons who play. One wraps up a part of his sticks in grass, the other matches a part of his to them. If they agree in number or colour of the lines, the one that matches wins five, or otherwise loses the same number. The game is always forty.

On the 18th of May, several parties of Indians arrived from the river Chein, for the purpose of trading, consisting of Dog Indians, *Gens-dis-valch*, *Kaewas*, and *Kales*. A trader likewise came in from the Assinniboin river. They all assembled at the village, at the mouth of the Warriuna river, and our camp moved up to the same village. The trader soon procured what furs of any value they had to dispose of, and departed. Mr. Pardo, having procured a supply of ammunition, proposed to ascend the Missouri, on a hunting expedition with a party of *Grossventres**, with whom he was connected by marriage. His wife was the daughter of the chief of this nation. He applied to the chief of our camp, to whom I belonged, whose name is Man-di-tongue-go, for liberty for me to accompany him. The chief consented that I should go with him, on condition that I should give him a part of the skins I procured, and lent me an old musket. There were three of

* This name has been spelt wrong and altered, but still wrong. The true spelling is found to be *Gross-Vantres*, or *Grossventres*. Also, Assinniboin river, is the true spelling.

the Sioux, one of whom was his relation, who agreed to go with us.

We started on the 27th of May, crossed Missouri, and arrived the same evening at the upper village. This village is situated on an Island, in the Missouri, and is fortified in the same manner as the lower village, containing about sixty huts. Our party consisted of twenty-seven men, six women, and four children; none of the Gross-Ventres having their families with them. The next morning we proceeded, and soon left the Missouri, travelling a northwest course, in a well beaten path. The land on each side of us ascended into high ridges. On the northern side of them, was considerable timber, mostly cedar, and the land poor. The path continued up the vally, but often passing over low ridges. On the 29th, we struck a branch of the stream called by the traders, Ball river. We followed this branch to its mouth. Here we crossed Ball river. We found some pleasant intervals on this river, but most of the land is poor, dry ridges, with very little timber. Our company soon took a course more northwardly, until we came to the mouth of Chuss-chu river. Here we came again to the banks of the Missouri, and met a party of Mandans, hunting buffaloe. The principal game found here is the buffaloe, cabree, or antelope, black tailed deer, and elk. We now frequently passed camps of Mandans, and on the 5th of June, arrived at the lower *Mandan* village. This village, which is above the great bend of the Missouri, is situated on a pleasant interval, covered with cotton wood and cedar. Is built and fortified in the same manner as those of the Rus.

Here a sight, new to me, and exceedingly disagreeable, arrested my attention as soon as I came in view of the village. This was their manner of depositing the bodies of the dead. Immediately after my arrival I had an opportunity of witnessing the funeral ceremonies practised by these people, which was in the following manner. A dead body was brought out of a hut, and laid on the ground before it, dressed in its best apparel, and wrapped in a buffaloe robe. The relations and principal part of the people in the village, assembled around it. A fire was then made, and the sacred stem, or pipe, was brought and lighted. The deceased having been a warrior, an eulogy of considerable length was pronounced by his brother, in which he impressed on their minds, the great importance which the deceased man had been to their nation; rehearsed his war exploits, and concluded by urging all to follow his example, and to become of equal usefulness to their tribe. Then they would be sure of following and becoming companions of him, and all the other great warriors, which had died before, in the world of spirits. After this address was closed, provisions were brought out, consisting of boiled dog's flesh, of which the company just tasted, and then a bowl full of it was presented to the dead man. He was then taken up by four men and carried outside of the village, just into the edge of the woods, and placed on a stage which had been previously erected, about ten feet high. The bowl of food was brought and set by his head, and his arms and accoutrements laid by his side. In this manner their dead are deposited, and are never buried. The wife and relations of the deceased made the most violent and dreadful howlings, tearing their hair, and appearing to be in the deepest anguish, under the loss they had sustained.

The Mandans and Gross-Ventres are of the lightest complexion, and largest Indians on the Missouri. Their hair inclines to a chesnut colour, and in some instances has a slight curl; it is never so lank and coarse as most other Indians. Their eyes are full and lively, their cheek bones rather high, and their countenances open and agreeable. The Gross-Ventres have more of a fierce, savage look, than the Mandans who are courteous and sociable in their behaviour. They are neat in their dress, which is similar to that of the Rus, excepting that they decorate it with white rabbit, and white ermine skins. Many of their lodges, or huts, are decorated in a beautiful manner; having the inside lined with the richest furs, such as the lynx, beaver, otter, white rabbit, martin, fox, mountain cat, and white ermine, sewed together like patch work, which gives them a rich and beautiful appearance. The lodge of the head chief was sixty feet in diameter, elegantly lined with furs, and the seats, which are also used as beds, were covered with the grizzly bear and buffaloe skins. These people keep their lodges and buildings in a state of great neatness. They cultivate the same kind of produce with the Rus, and carry on a trade with the roving Indians, who occasionally visit them. The Mandans and Gross-Ventres live in great friendship, although they speak different languages; and it is necessary they should, for their villages are not more than six miles apart. The Mandans speak the same tongue of the Osage, but have a different accent, and dialect. They were once a numerous, warlike people, but have been reduced by the small pox, and by their enemies, the Sioux, to less than four hundred warriors.

On the the 13th, we left the Mandans, and arrived at the Gross-Ventres village, which is on the lower side of Batteau river, and is called the *Meniture* village. Another village, called *Menitar-u-miti-ha-tah*, is situated on the upper side of Batteau river. These villages are larger than the Mandans, built in the same manner, and containing about six hundred warriors, and about twenty-five hundred inhabitants. They were formerly more numerous, but the small pox has made its ravages among them. These people deposit their dead in the same manner as the Mandans, but at a greater distance from their villages. Soon after our arrival, a young chief, who accompanied us, found a young woman, with whom he contracted matrimony, which afforded an opportunity to witness their marriage ceremonies. Proclamation was made, by one of the relations, that on the next day, in the morning, the marriage would be celebrated. The next morning the bride was dressed in all her finery, and the groom in his richest attire. The company assembled at her father's lodge, where the chief of the village attended. He informed the company, that the young man, calling him by name, intended to take the girl, calling her by name, to be his wife. He then asked each of them if that were their intention, which each of them answered in the affirmative. The chief then handed them a small rod, which was broken between them. The groom then broke his part into a number of small pieces, and handed them to the men who stood near to him. The bride did the same with her part of the rod, which consumated the marriage. Fire was then brought, and the sacred pipe was lighted. After all the men had smoked in it, the dance commenced, which was continued for several hours. As soon as it was finished, the groom took his bride to his lodge to live with him.

These people entertain ideas of chastity very different from any civilized nation. If a stranger comes to reside with them in their cabins, for several days, he is presented with the wife or a daughter to be his bed-fellow, during his stay. If a girl proves with child, it has no influence to prevent her marriage, and the child is adopted by her husband, and brought up as his own. Their hospitality probably exceeds that of any other people. They share the last mouth full of provisions chearfully, with the greatest stranger, and strive to make him as happy and contented as possible.

Our party now prepared to set out for the summer and fall hunt, and it was determined to go to the River Jaun or Yellow Stone, and to the Rocky mountain. All things being prepared to set off, the 2d of July was assigned, as is usual among these people, for a day of feasting. The feast was prepared, and the ceremonies conducted in the same manner, as at the Rus village, which has been described. After the smoking rite was finished, the head chief of the village addressed us. He commended us to the care of the Great Spirit, and all the good subordinate spirits, wishing us a bright sun and clear sky, that we might overcome any enemy we might meet; that the evil spirits would not spread sickness among us, and that all of us, in due season, should return to the village, loaded with meat and skins. The day was closed with feasting and dancing.

On the 3d of July, the party assembled to the number of forty-three men, women and children; nineteen of whom were men, besides Mr. Pardo and myself. We were provided with thirty-six

16*

horses, one I had hired for myself, and Mr. Pardo had two for himself and squaw. About noon we left the village, and proceeded up the Batteau river, until we passed the second large fork, and then we crossed it to the north side. The river here was about an hundred yards wide, and fordable. The country was barren and hilly. On the 7th, we came to Salt springs, where buffaloe and cabree were very plenty; and the country much infested with wolves, which were very ravenous. Some Indians had very lately removed from this place. We supposed them to have been some of the *Gens-di-foulers*, who live three miles below the Gross-Ventres, on the Missouri. We occupied their camp, and continued here until the 9th, when we proceeded a western course, crossing a barren country destitute of timber. On the 10th, we came to a branch of the Jaun, called Road river, and followed this branch down to its mouth; where, on the 15th, we arrived at the River Jaun, and encamped in a cotton wood grove. The country near the Jaun is more level, and some of the intervals are very rich; but large barren hills are to be seen at a distance from the river. A party of the *Gens-des-corbeau*, or Crow Indians, had lately encamped at this place, and their tent poles accommodated us. The river is about half a mile wide, and shallow, but not fordable. We supposed ourselves about a hundred miles from the mouth. Here we caught a number of very fine fish, mostly pike and cat. On the

ROCKY-MOUNTAIN SHEEP.

18th, we crossed the Jaun, and passed up to the mouth of the stream, called by the Indians, *La-ca-sha-newatu*, or Crooked river, where, on the 19th, we encamped.

The Jaun is a noble stream, somewhat rapid, the bottom sandy, and the water clear; excepting when rain falls, and then it becomes immediately thick from the earth that is washed into it from the barren hills. Many of these hills are so washed, and become so steep, that no animal can ascend them, except the cabree and mountain ram, or rocky mountain sheep. The grizzly or white bear, is plenty in this country, and often attacks the natives. We continued at this camp until the 29th, and then proceeded up Crooked river, and encamped near the first ridge of mountains. Here we killed several of these rocky mountain sheep. The male is considerably larger than the female, and has much longer horns. The horns of a male which we killed, measured three feet in length, and five inches diameter, at his head. This animal is taller than a deer, and has a larger body. It is covered with soft hair of a dun colour, gradually becoming of a lighter colour towards the belly, which is entirely white. Its horns are shaped, in every respect, like the horns of rams, of the common sheep, bending backwards, but have many rough knobs. Its tail resembles that of the red deer. The legs and feet resemble the sheep, but the hoofs some what longer. It is swift and climbs the clifts of rocks with so much agility and ease, that no other animal can follow it; and by this means it escapes the wolves. Its flesh is esteemed equal to that of the deer.

On the 3d of August, we moved up into the mountains and met with a camp of *Gens-de-panse*, or the Paunched Indians. We encamped with them for the night, and on the 4th, about noon, we had like to have been defeated, by a monstrous white bear. Four or five of the men were ahead, and turning the point of a steep hill, they met a white bear, and fired upon him, but only wounded him. He immediately turned upon them, and they retreated. At the point of the hill they met the rest of the party, the bear pursuing close to their heels, which threw the whole party into confusion. Not being room for us to escape, the bear was in a moment in the midst of us. As one man turned and attempted to run, the bear seized his buffaloe robe, and had not the fastening given way, would have drawn him under his paws. While he was spending his rage on the robe, one of the men shot him dead on the spot. As soon as he fell, the whole party made the air ring with their shouts. This bear was much larger than the black bear. The meat only would have weighed more than four hundred pounds. The mountains here are steep, and some of their points and sides are covered with a small growth, mostly of the spruce kind. The stream we were ascending is winding, interrupted, and full of rapids, but it is about one hundred yards wide. We encamped in a large interval, at the mouth of a small stream, and continued here until the 12th. The fur animals had now just done shedding, so that we only hunted the buffaloe, cabree, and mountain sheep. A party was sent to gain the summit of a ridge, so as to pass over to the other side, while the rest of us crawled up, surrounding them on every side, excepting towards the river. As soon as the signal was given, by those who had ascended and gained the opposite side, we all raised a sudden yell, and sprang out of the grass, and the affrighted animals instantly fled from us, pitched over the precipice, and were dashed against the stones, at the bottom, where we killed sixty-one. Some of them fell nearly two hundred feet; but some of them, which were near the bottom, made their escape. It took us several days to dress and cure the meat. The method in which these people cure their meat is to cut it into thin slices, and dry it by the heat of the sun, or a slow fire. They use no salt to preserve it. Meat will continue in this state, if well dried, for a long time. We killed a wild cat, which resembled the domestic cat, and was of about the same size. It was of a sallow colour, and had a tail nearly of the length of the body. This little animal is very fierce, and often kills cabree and sheep, by jumping on their necks, and eating away the sinews and arteries until they fall, and then sucks the blood. On the 25th, we proceeded up, eighteen miles, to the mouth of a large fork of the river, which comes from the north, and encamped on a plain. At this encampment, the snow-topped mountains appeared to be at no great distance. Here we found beaver in plenty; and as the fur had become good, we began to trap them. One of the Indians killed a beautiful wild cat, about one half larger than the house cat. Its fur was long and exceedingly fine, covered with black and white spots on a bright yellow ground. Its belly was pale yellow, and its tail about two inches long. It is the richest looking skin I ever saw. On the 28th, we killed two grizzly bears. In the evening we had a severe storm of hail, and the hail stones which fell were larger than musket balls. Here the mountain sheep are plenty, but they keep mostly on high ridges and the tops of the inaccessible mountains. On the 30th, moved further up the river, and caught a number of the lynx, marten and ermine. The ermine is a beautiful little animal, as white as milk, except the tip of the tail, which is of a jet black. On the 2d of September, had a heavy shower of snow, after which we returned to our encampment of the 28th of August. We continued trapping here until the 12th, when we crossed the river, took a branch which comes from the southward, and followed it up about six miles, where we encamped in a small bottom. Here we found fur plenty, and caught a number of beaver, otter, marten, ermine, and two spotted wild cats.

Buffaloe were plenty, but as we had secured as much meat as we could carry, we seldom troubled them. On the 16th, we proceeded about ten miles further, and continued here until the 24th, when having loaded our horses, we crossed over a mountain, and encamped on a branch of Big-horn river. The weather was cold, and frequent showers of snow made the travelling difficult. Here the stream was rapid, about thirty yards wide, and winding its way amongst the steep mountains. We were however obliged frequently to cross it ourselves, with our horses loaded with as much as they could carry. On the 28th, we came to a camp of the Crow Indians, where we rested until the 30th, when we continued our course down the river.

The Crow Indians speak either the Mandan or Gross-Ventres tongue, or both of those languages. They left the camp and accompanied us. Here we found the travelling less difficult than it had been. On the 3d of October, we passed two camps, and on the 5th, several more camps, on our way to Big-horn river, where we arrived at night. On the south side is a winter camp of the Crow Indians, consisting of forty-three huts. These huts were sunk three feet below the surface of the ground, but otherwise are built nearly similar to those of the Gross-Ventres. In the centre a post is erected, with notches cut in it for steps, and a hole is left open at the top of it, sufficiently large for a man to crawl out, which is their passage out and in, during the winter. At this encampment we prepared our buffaloe skin canoes, to descend the Big-horn river, which is large, being three hundred yards wide, with a strong current. On the 9th, we embarked, for the mouth of the river, having detached eight Indians to proceed with the horses by land. At night we stopped at a camp of Crow Indians. Early in the morning of the 10th, we again proceeded, the current very rapid, and at night encamped. On the 11th, we proceeded early, and at night, arrived at the mouth of the river. Here is a village of Crow Indians, but of a different band from those we met with in the mountains. The Crow Indians are divided into four bands, which they distinguish by the following names, *Ah-hah-hee-no-pah. Nootsa-pah-zasah, Keet-keet-sah,* and *Ehart-sah.* This village belongs to the *Nootsa-pah-zasah* band. The band we had left was the *Keet-keet-sah,* and is the largest of them, consisting of two hundred warriors. The band here consists of one hundred and sixty warriors. This band had lately been on a war expedition against a nation of Indians, who reside on the west side of Rocky mountains, called *Pal-lo-to-path,* or Flat-heads, and had returned with sixteen prisoners, and a number of scalps.

The Flat-heads have a singular practice of flattening their heads, which is different from any other nation of Indianes in this country. It is effected in the following manner. Soon after an

A MAN of the FLAT-HEAD NATION.

infant is born, two boards are prepared, by drawing a dressed skin over them. One board is longer than the other, and the longest is placed on the back part of the head, extending from the neck about eight inches above the head; the shortest board is placed against the forehead, from the eyebrows, and meets the upper end of the other board. It is then laced together at the sides, and the head of the child is thus confined between these boards, until the child has grown to a considerable bigness. After the head is become sufficiently flattened, it is taken out of this compress. One of the prisoners had her infant child with its head in the frame. I also saw some of the prisoners which were two or three years old, who, I was informed, had the frame on when they were taken. This compression forms the head into the shape of a wedge, swelling it out over the ears, and gives the head a very singular shape. These people are of a middle stature, well formed, and of a pleasant countenance. Their skin of an olive colour, hair lank and coarse, and ther features regular and handsome. The men had a bone passed through the gristle of the nose, which separates the nostril, that extended the width of the face. All the hair on their heads was pulled out, except a lock on the crown, which was left to grow its full length. This tuft of hair was divided into two parts, tied up in a short cue, **and fell over each ear. Their dress consisted of nothing more than leggins and moccasons, ex-**

cepting a young chief, who had a belt of white ermine skins round his middle, and a necklace of white bear's claws around his neck. All the men were tattooed on the breast, with two long, and one short line, drawn horizontally, but on no other part of the body. The women wear their hair tied up in two clubs, which hang over each ear, and a long braid down the back. They were not tattooed, nor do they wear any ornaments, except beads of their own make, formed out of sea shells, about the size of a barberry. Their dress consisted of a buffaloe robe, or a mountain sheep skin, thrown over their shoulders, ground hog skins sewed together, with the tails hanging out on the fur side, fastened round their middle with a belt of raw hide.

On the 13th, a large party of Snake Indians arrived. This nation resides principally on the head waters of the Big-horn river, and in the most inaccessible parts of the rocky mountains, where they have frequently to hide in caverns from their enemies. Owing to their defenceless situation, they become an easy conquest to any nation disposed to attack them; and they are frequently attacked for no other reason, than the pleasure of killing them. Their appearance bespoke their distressed situation to which they are reduced. The complexion of these Indians is dark, but their features are regular, although their visage is thin, and their eyes pretty much sunk into their heads. Their bodies are frequently

A WOMAN of the FLAT-HEAD NATION,
& a Child with its head in the Frame.

crooked, a thing very rarely to be seen among Indians; of a small size, thin and slender. Both men and women have their hair hanging loose on their heads, and only cut short over their eyes. Their dress consists only of mountain sheep, cabree or deer skins, thrown over their shoulders. The women sometimes wore a girdle of loose bark, tied round their middle, which was but an indifferent covering. Their ornaments consisted of white bear's claws, and a few beads. The men were armed with the *Casoe-tite*, or war club, a target or shield made of raw buffaloe hides, a dagger made of bone, ten inches long, and a small bow. We were the first white people which either they, or the Flat-heads had ever seen. The Flat-heads, likewise, arm themselves with the war club, in which a bone is fastened that projects three inches, a bone dagger, and sometimes one made of iron, which they work out themselves, ten inches long, and three wide, at the handle; a spear pointed with bone or iron, and when they cross the mountains to hunt the buffaloe, they carry a bow with them. The buffaloe is not found on the west side of the Rocky mountains, and there these people subsist on fish and roots.

Our horses arrived on the 15th, and on the 16th, we embarked, to ascend the Jaun river. On the 17th, came to a camp of the Paunch Indians, where we halted for the horses. These Indians reside mostly towards the head waters of the river Jaun, and the branches of the Big-horn.

They are a large, well looking people, somewhat inclined to corpulency. From this circumstance they have acquired the name of *Gens-de-Panse*, but they call themselves *All-ah-kaa-wiah*. They speak a different language from the Gross-Ventres. Their arms consist of bows and spears, with buffaloe skin targets, much larger than those made use of by the Snake Indians, and so thick and firm that an arrow will not pierce them. They use a short bone dagger, and the war club. A few of them had guns, but no ammunition. Many of the Crow Indians and Gross-Ventres, are armed in the same manner.

On the 18th, our horses arrived, and we proceeded, passing many camps of Indians, and halted at night on an island, where we killed a large white bear. The river is rapid but has no obstruction. The ice now began to float, which rendered our navigation dangerous in such slight vessels. Here the Rocky mountains may be seen at a distance to the westward; but the land near the river is mostly level, and though destitute of timber, is apparently of a good soil. The general course of the river is to the north, and sometimes west of north. On the 22d, we arrived at the mouth of a large branch which comes from the southeast, and encamped to wait for the horses. About six miles up this branch, a party of Crow Indians were encamped, and intended to spend the winter. On the 25th, the horses arrived, and as the ice ran thick, took out our boats, and encamped for the winter. Our encampment was in a grove of cotton wood, and willows, and we formed as comfortable huts as possible. Mr. Pardo and myself built one for our own accommodation, with one adjoining for our horses.

On the 3d of November, the buffaloes descended from the mountains in vast droves. The plains were covered with them and with elk. The Indians hunt the buffaloe on horse back, with a bow and a short spear. They ride as near as possible to the gang, and discharge their arrows, while the animals are fighting their dogs. A wounded buffaloe, if he does not fall, frequently turns upon the hunter, who depends upon the dexterity of his horse, which has been trained up to the business, for his escape. He then discharges more arrows, and dispatches the animal with his spear. These hunts are attended with considerable danger, and sometimes with the loss of both horse and rider. The country in which we were encamped is level to the south, but to the north and west the mountains are in sight, with steep ridges, approaching the river; and to the east is a large mountain, entirely insulated from the Rocky mountains, called the *Turtle.* This mountain, with the country round it, is covered with timber. Large bands of Indians encamp near it, during the winter for the conveniency of wood. In some places wood is so scarce that they perish with cold, for want of it.

The extensive country on the Jaun, or Yellow river, is exceedingly fertile. Towards its head waters the land is covered with large timber. Grapes grow in great abundance wherever any trees or brush are to be found. There are vast thickets of plumbs, cherries, and crab-apples. The country is mostly level to the foot of the Black mountains, which the Indians say, are completely separated from Rocky mountains. A large river passes between them, which runs to the southward. The range of the Black mountains is from east to west, but the Rocky mountains extend from north to south. The former are about four hundred miles south of our winter encampment, as the Indians compute the distance. They represent the country as fertile beyond description, and as inhabited by numerous bands of Indians. The buffaloe, elk, cabree, deer, black and white bears, are found there, in vast multitudes. The *Manclarie* Indians are often at war with a nation, which resides in the Black mountains, called, *J-a-kar-tha*, who speak the same tongue with the Snake Indians or the *Aliatans* of the Rocky mountains. This nation has also obtained the nick name of Snake Indians, from the same circumstance; that is, because they hide themselves in caverns and among the rocks, to conceal themselves from their enemies, from whence they are dragged out and killed like snakes. They are also held in great contempt by other nations, who consider them to be too mean to have existence.

The Indians say, that vast numbers of horses and mules abound in, and about the Black mountains. Towards the mouth of the River Jaun, the country is open, level, with extensive prairies, or natural meadows, covered with high grass, but no wood, excepting cotton wood, willows, and a few cedars. On the north side of the Missouri, near the Rocky mountains, resides a nation of Indians, who are numerous, and who are the inveterate enemies of the Gross-Ventres and Crow Indians, and frequently fall on their hunting parties. Their are called Black-foot Indians. I saw one of this nation, who was a prisoner taken by the Crow Indians. He was a large, well made, and his complexion as light as the Gross-Ventres. They are a roving nation, have no villages, nor do they raise any kind of produce.

The weather becoming mild, on the 12th of March, 1803, we moved up the river on which we had encamped, called by the Indians *Nan-tu-se-car*, or Stillwater river, which is about sixty yards wide. On the 15th, came to salt springs, and boiled some of the water. On the 18th, procured a small quantity of salt, which, to me, was a great relief, as I had lost my appetite for want of it; not having tasted any for more than three months. On the 19th, moved our encampment on to high land, the Salt springs being in a low interval, to avoid the water produced by the melting of the snow. Here the Turtle mountain appeared at a great distance, in a southeast direction. On the 24th, the snow fell about a foot deep. We proceeded in a northerly direction, and encamped, at night, on a small stream, and continued to the 30th, owing to the fleet and rain. On the 30th, we continued our course, in the same direction, through a plain country, in a well beaten path, and on the 4th of April, came to a branch of the Still-water river, where we encamped to hunt. On the 8th, caught several beaver, otter, and white rabits, which were very numerous. On the 12th, we arrived at the river, we had ascended in July, called Road river, and on the 13th, came to the Salt springs, where we procured a small quantity more of salt. On the 18th, proceeded to the mouth of Catteau, or Knife river, where we arrived on the 24th of April. On the 25th, a great feast was made with the usual ceremonies.

We left the upper Gross-Ventres village, on the 4th of May, in company with a large number of Indians for the trading post on the Assinniboin river, distant about one hundred miles, and on the 11th, arrived at the station. I had formed a determination to leave the Indians at this place, but was prevented by the Sioux Indians, who were with us. The Sioux Indian, who was a relation to the chief, was offered a musket, knife, and hatchet, if he would let me go, but he refused, declaring that I must go with him to his uncle. The traders not being willing to offend the Indians, I was obliged to remain with them. On the 5th of June, I parted with Mr. Pardo and my former companions, and went with a party of Sioux, of the *Tilon Okandanas* band, for the heads of Saint Peter's river. The chief, *Man-da-tonque-qua*, was gone with part of the *Bois-bruil* band. On the 15th, we came to a band of the *Bois-bruil*, on Saint Peter's river, but the chief was not with them. He had gone with a small party to meet a band of *Yanton-ansah* Sioux, who were proceeding from the falls of Saint Anthony, on the Mississippi, where they had been to procure merchandize, to trade with the other bands. The country we had lately passed through, was mostly level, swampy, and full of small lakes, covered very thick with timber, chiefly pine and spruce. On the 17th, we proceeded down the Saint Peter's, and on the 20th, came to the encampment. This body of Indians consisted of five bands; the *Yanton-ansah*, *Wah-pa-coo-ta*, *Titon-bois-bruil*, *Titon-okan-danas*, and *Titon-sa-oo-nu*, about four hundred warriors, and about one thousand four hundred people. On the 27th, the bands mostly separated, and the greater part returned to the Missouri, among whom was the *Bois-bruil* band, who took the war path. The greatest part of these Indians were well armed, and mounted on good horses, On the 12th of July, encamped at the forks of the River Sasqui, a branch of the Missouri, On the 18th, these bands separated, and we proceeded to the crossing of the three rivers, on the Missouri, above the mouth of White river. On the 8th of August, we arrived at the Missouri, and a party of us went down to the Salt springs, and made a quantity of salt. The water in the River Sasqui and in the Three rivers is so brackish, as to be very disagreeable to drink; and many other streams on the Missouri have a similar taste. On the 20th, we returned to the encampment and on the 28th, I went with a party up the Middle fork of the Three rivers, to hunt. The country is considerably broken, and destitute of timber; but numerous salt licks and a plenty of game. On the 16th of September, we returned, having loaded our horses.

We remained at this encampment until the 27th, when we moved up to Teton river. I obtained liberty, on the 3d of October, to go to the Rus village. Here I spent the winter with a number of traders belonging to Saint Louis. The Sioux are enemies to the traders, who follow this employment on the Missouri. They hold them in the greatest contempt, and always rob them whenever they can get a good opportunity.

On the 12th of April, 1804, the traders left the village, and went up the River Chein, or Dog river, to trade. The chief *Man-da-tonque-qua* came to the village, on the 18th, and took me with him on to the Sioux river, where we arrived on the 6th of May, and continued until the 12th of June, when we removed to the River Sasqui. On the 26th of August, a report was spread among the Indians, that a party, an army, as they called it, of soldiers were coming up the Missouri.* After dispatching messengers to all the Indians near, they hastened to the river, leaving all their women and children with a few men in the encampment. They did not permit me to go with them. On the 25th of September, a council was held on the River Sasqui, to deliberate on the object this army should have in view, and to determine what should be done. Lengthy debates took place, and being much divided in sentiment whether they should attack them, or not, they disolved the council on the 29th, without deciding what should be done. Another council was held on the 5th of November, consisting of a much larger number, when they came to a determination to invite the Rus to join them, and to attack the soldiers early in the spring. They also agreed to declare war against the Mandans and the Gross-Ventres. During the winter, large bodies of Indians assembled on the Sioux river and the River Sasqui, near to the Missouri.

In the mean time, war was declared against the soldiers and against the Mandans and Gross-Ventres. Early in the spring the spies they had

---

* The army reported to be coming up the Missouri, was doubtless, the party under the command of Captain Lewis and Captain Clarke, consisting of forty-five men, bound on a voyage of discovery to the Pacific Ocean. This corps entered the Missouri on the 14th of May, 1804, and passed the mouth of the River Sasqui, about the 28th of August.

sent out, reported that the soldiers had gone further up the river, so that on the 4th of April, 1805, our camp, with the women and children, moved on to the Missouri. Immediately after I arrived here, I was so fortunate as to become acquainted with Mr. Paintille, a Frenchman, who had long resided in the country, principally with the *Titon-anah* band of Sioux. We concerted a plan for making an escape down the Missouri. As he had a light canoe, we prepared ourselves to leave the Indians, and accordingly, on the night of the 26th of April, we were so happy as to make our escape from these miserable beings. In ten days we arrived at the town of Saint John's, which is the upper settlement on the Missouri river, and from thence we proceeded to the lower settlements. Here I found myself in the full enjoyment of a freedom, of which I had long been deprived; having been a prisoner more than three years and six months. During this period I had been subjected to many severe sufferings. Although I had always been well treated by the Indians, I had undergone great fatigues, and was often much distressed for provisions. Frequent exposure to wet and cold, and the inclemency of weather, brought on a rheumatism, which became so severe, as to confine me eighteen months after I had obtained my liberty.

APPENDIX.

As an historical sketch has been given of the Indian nations, within what is considered the limits of Louisiana, on the western side of the river Mississippi, it is presumed that some account of the natives residing west of the Alleghany mountains, and in the vicinity of the lakes, would be acceptable. The following is given from the best materials the writer was able to procure. To ascertain the numbers of each nation, with any great degree of precision, is impracticable. They are taken principally from former estimates, since which individual nations have doubtless considerably varied in number. Since the close of the American revolutionary war, some of the nations have increased in population, while others have diminished. Mr. Imlay, in his history of Kentucky, estimates the whole number of Indians, from the gulph of Mexico, on both sides the Mississippi, to its head waters, to the gulph of Saint Lawrence; and as far west as the country has been explored, between the Missouri and Saint a Fè; to be only 60,000 souls. This estimation must be much less than their real number. Mr. Purcell, who resided among the Indians, computes only the Creeks, Chacktaws, Chickasaws, Cherokees, and Catabaws, in the year 1780, to consist of 13,516 warriors, and 42,033 souls. The roving life and frequent migrations of the natives, increase the difficulty of ascertaining the number of particular nations. Tribes and small bands often separate from their nation, and form confederacies with others, or find some new place of residence. After the establishment of peace by General Wayne, at Greenville, in 1795, at which time large tracts of land were ceded to the United States, nearly all the Indians who resided on the lands, to which their claims were extinguished, retread back, and found new places of residence.

The most northern and eastern nations, near the lakes, are the Six Nations. They have been so called by the English and Americans, but the French styled them *Irquois*. They call themselves *Aganuschioni*, which in their language, signifies the *United People*. This confederacy, which consisted at first of only five nations, is of ancient date. The nations who first united were the Mohawks, Oneidas, Onondagas, Senecas, and Cayugas. About eighty years ago they were joined by the Tuscaroras. The Mohawks were formerly at the head of the confederacy, and were a very powerful nation. They inhabited on Mohawk river. The old Mohawk town was at the mouth of Schohary creek, twelve miles west of Schenectady, which was not entirely abandoned until 1780. Here is still the remains of an old church, built in the reign of Queen Ann. They were strongly attached to Sir William Johnson, and the Johnson family. About 300 went with Sir John Johnson, to Canada in 1776, and reside in Upper Canada, on the northern waters of Lake Erie.

At the time of the American revolution, the Six Nations were in alliance with the English, engaged on their side, and made great depredations on the frontiers. In the year 1779, the American troops gained a complete victory over them, and destroyed all their towns. By a treaty at Fort Stanwix, in 1784, a tract of land was assigned them, bordering on Lake Erie and Ontario, and a quantity of goods given them for their use and comfort. And by a subsequent treaty, at Konon-daigua, in 1794, their boundary lines were varied, in conformity to treaties they had made with the State of New York, and the tract confirmed to them by the United States. This tract is called the *State Reservation*, on which they now reside. In consideration of the extinguishment of their claims to other lands, and to secure perpetuate peace and friendship, the United States delivered to the Six Nations, and to the Indians of other nations, residing among them, and united with them, a quantity of goods to the value of 10,000 dollars, and stipulated an annuity of 4,500 dollars, to be expended yearly, forever, in purchasing clothing, domestic animals, implements of husbandry, and in compensating useful artificers, who shall reside with, or near them, and be employed for their benefit. All the Mohawks and a considerable part of the Cayugas have migrated to Canada. It is thought probable they will all quit the United States, and retire over the Lakes Ontario and Erie, and settle with their former associates. There is an exact census of all these Indians taken annually. The number of souls, in 1796, exclusive of the Mohawks and Cayugas moved into Canada, was 3,298. The Stockbridge and Brotherton Indians, who are united with them and reside among them, are 1,210, making the whole number of the Six Nations 4,508 souls. They can probably furnish about 1,400 warriors.

The Sachems, chiefs and warriors of the following nations and tribes, having met together at Greenville, on a branch of the Great Miami, General Wayne concluded a treaty of peace, harmony, and friendly intercourse between the United States, and these Indians, on the 3d day of August 1795. The nations and tribes were the Wyandots, Delawares, Shawanoes, Ottawas, Chippewas, Ottawa from Sandusky lake, Putawatames of the River Saint Joseph, Putawatames of Huron, Miamies, and Eel-river, Eel-river tribe, Miamis, Weeas for themselves and the Piankashow, Kikapoos, Kaskaskias, and Delawares of Sandusky. By the third article of the treaty, a general boundary line between the lands of the United States, and the lands of the said Indian tribes, was established. All the land lying eastwardly and southwardly of the general boundary line. These tribes ceded to the United States, and relinquished all their claims forever. They also made a cession of sixteen pieces of land, of different dimensions, and at different places, within their own line, as an evidence of returning friendship, and to provide for the accommodation, convenient intercourse, and mutual benefit of both parties. In addition to these cessions, the said tribes relinquished all title and claim which they, or any of them, may have to the tract of 150,000 acres, near the rapids of the Ohio river, which has been assigned to

General Clark and his warriors; a tract of land adjacent to post Saint Vicennes, on the Wabash, to which the Indian title had been extinguished; the land at all other places in possession of the French people and other white settlers among them, of which the Indian title had been extinguished; and a tract at Fort Massac, towards the mouth of the Ohio.

In consideration of these cessions, and with a view to preserve peace and a friendly intercourse, the United States delivered to these tribes a quantity of goods, of the value of 20,000 dollars, and are hence forwarded every year forever, to deliver them like useful goods, suited to the circumstances of the Indians, to the amount of 9,500 dollars, valued at the place where they are procured. These goods are to be delivered in the following proportions; to the Wyandots, the value of 1,000 dollars; to the Delawares, 1,000 dollars; to the Shawanese, 1,000 dollars; to the Miamis, 1,000 dollars; to the Attawas, 1,000 dollars; to the Chippewas 1,000 dollars; to the Putawatimes, 1,000 dollars; and to the Kickapoos, Weeas, Eel-river, Piankashaws, and Kaskaskias tribes, 500 dollars each.

The Wyandots inhabit the country near the river Saint Joseph and Fort Detroit, and have their hunting ground about the western end of Lake Erie. Their warriors, some years ago were two hundred and fifty, and the number of souls estimated at about 800. A tribe of the Wyandots, reside near Sandusky, in the neighbourhood of a tribe of the Mohickons and Coghnawagas. The warriors of these three tribes were, a number of years ago, three hundred, and the inhabitants about 1,000.

The Delaware nation emigrated from the northern parts of Pennsylvania and New-Jersey, and probably received their name from their residence on the Delaware river. The name by which they called themselves was *Linnilenape,* which, in their language, signifies *Indian Men.* They were formerly a very numerous and powerful nation, but are much reduced. Before the settlements commenced in the State of Ohio, their villages were about midway between the

Ohio river and Lake Erie, on the Muskingum, and on the branches of Beaver Creek and Guyehago, but they have since retired to the country about Lake Erie. They are naturally ingenious, intelligent and of a peacable disposition, rarely contending with any of the neighbouring Indian tribes. Lately they were hostile to the Americans, and committed depredations. The number of their warriors has been computed to be six hundred, and their number of souls about 2,000.

The Shawanoes resided on the head waters of the Scioto and the northern branches of the Muskingum, but they are now on Stone creek, which empties into the Great Miami, and at the Miami villages. They have been able to raise three hundred warriors. Parts of this nation have emigrated to the southward of the Ohio river, and joined the Creek confederacy. It has been said of the Shawanoes that they are generally handsome featured, of a rather small size, and a very chearful, crafty people : that counselling among the old people, and dancing among their young men and women, occupies a great portion of their time.

The Ottawa nation is divided into several tribes or bands. The largest part of the nation live not far distant from Detroit, and hunt about Lake Erie, and some time past, could raise four hundred warriors. Another part resides on the eastern side of Lake Michigan, about twenty miles southward of Michilimackinack. Their hunting ground is between this lake and Lake Huron. They have been able to furnish about two hundred warriors. One of the tribes live near the Chippewas, on Saguinam bay, who, together had two hundred warriors. Another tribe resides near Fort Saint Joseph, and have about one hundred and fifty warriors. And one other small band live near Sandusky, who are supposed to have not more than about fifty warriors.

The Chippewas are a very numerous nation, divided into a vast number of tribes and bands, which are scattered over a tract country represented by M'Kenzie, to extend two thousand miles. Some of them reside on Lake Huron; others on the borders of Lake Superior, on the Chippeway riv-

18*

er, on both sides of Mississippi; and as far to the westward as the Assinniboin river. Very little appears to be known of the numbers which compose this nation. The tribes inhabiting the coasts and islands of Lake Superior, according to Hutchins, can furnish one thousand warriors. Those residing in the country about Saguinam and Puan bays, and on the borders of Huron and Machigan, together with the tribes of Saukees and Mynomanies, who live near them, are estimated at five hundred and fifty warriors. These last mentioned tribes were hostile to the United States, and signed the treaty at Greenville.

The Putanotimes consist of two tribes, one of which resides on the River Saint Joseph, and the other near Detroit. Their warriors are estimated at about five hundred. These tribes were both hostile to the United States, and were parties in the treaty at Greenville.

The Miamies who signed the Greenville treaty, (it is presumed) include those only who inhabit the village of that name near the Miami Fort. Their number of warriors is unknown.

The Miamis nation live on the Miami of the lakes, and on lands southward of Lake Michigan. They can furnish about three hundred warriors.

The Eel-river Indians reside on a river of that name, which is a head branch of the Wabash. Their number of warriors cannot be ascertained.

Kathtippacamunch was an Indian village, situated on the north side of the Wabash river, at the mouth of Tippacanoe creek, about twenty miles above the lower Weeatowns. In 1791, before it was destroyed by Generals Scott and Wilkinson, it is said to have "contained one hundred and twenty houses, eighty of which were shingle roofed. The best houses belonged to the French traders. The gardens and improvements round were delightful. There was a tavern with cellars, bar, public and private rooms; and the whole marked no small degree of order and civilization."

Not far distant from the mouth of Tippacanoe creek, is the town of the much famed Indian Prophet, who is said to be a Shawanoes.

The Piankashaws, Kickapoos, Musquitons, and Ouiatanos, are tribes on the branches of the Wabash and Illinois rivers. They could raise, according to Hutchins, one thousand warriors. Other tribes of the Kickapoos reside at the entrance of Lake Superior, and could raise four hundred warriors. Another tribe inhabits with the Otutagamies, and Musquateys, between Michigan and the Mississippi, who together had one thousand warriors.

The Naudowesies live between Michigan and Lake Superior, and have five hundred warriors. The Killistinoes on Lake Superior, and have two hundred and fifty warriors. Mingoes on the Scioto, and have fifty warriors. Lezars between the Wabash and the mouth of the Ohio. The greater part of these Indians have taken up new places of residence. They had three hundred warriors. Outimaes, between Michigan and Lake Saint Clair. Warriors two hundred. Winnebagoes inhabit about the Lake of the same name, south of Green bay. Their village is situated on an island near the end of the lake, and can raise about three hundred warriors. Illinois tribe inhabit a village near Cahokia river on the Mississippi, and can furnish two hundred and sixty warriors. There are a number of other tribes, towns and villages, north of the River Ohio, within the boundaries of the United States; especially in the extensive country between the Illinois river and the Upper lakes. But the deficiency of information is too great to attempt any description of them.

South of the Ohio, the Cherokee nation inhabit a tract of country lying in the southern parts of Tennessee, and northern parts of Georgia, being separated on the east from North and South Carolina, by the Apalachian or Cherokee mountains, and extending on the west, to Duck river, running into the Tennessee. By a tract concluded between the United States and the Cherokee nation, at Hopewell, in November, 1785, the boundary between the citizens of the United States, and the country allotted to this nation for hunting ground is particularly designated. The Cherokees have been a famous Indian nation, but is now on the decline. Frequent wars with the northern tribes, and with white people, have greatly reduced their numbers. They are said to have had two thousand five hundred warriors, but they are now estimated at one thousand five hundred. They have about forty-five towns in which they reside when they are not engaged in hunting or war excursions. They are a tall, robust, and well formed people, of a lighter complexion than the neighbouring Indian nations. The men are very generally six feet in height. The women are also tall and of an handsome figure, rather slender and delicate. This nation has been much celebrated for their talents and correct morals.

The Chickasaws reside in the Mississippi Territory, on the Yazoo river, and westward of the Tennessee river, as far north as the Ohio, of and down the Ohio and Mississippi, to the Chactaw line of Natchez district. The boundary of the lands allotted to this nation is particularly described in the treaty of Hopewell on the 10th of January, 1786. Their country lies north of the Chactaw nation, and is very much an extended plain with little rising land. It is well watered and the soil generally good. They reside in about seven or eight towns and had formerly five hundred and seventy-five warriors, and seventeen hundred and twenty-five souls.

The Chactaws, a powerful, subtle, hardy, Indian nation, reside between the Tombigby and Mississippi rivers. The limits of the country, within the United States on which this nation is to live and hunt, was particularly stipulated at the treaty of Hopewell, on the 3d of January, 1786. Their country is hilly, with extensive, fertile plains intervening between the high lands. Unlike most of the Indian nations they have paid considerable attention to husbandry. Some of them have large farms, in a good state of culture, and many of them spend much of their time in agricultural improvements. Although they do not possess one quarter part of the quantity of land which the Creek nation occupies, their number of people is more than two thirds as large as the Creek confederacy. Many years ago they had forty-three towns and villages, containing 4,041 warriors, and 12,123 souls. Since that time they are supposed to have considerably increased in population. These people are said to be slovenly and dirty in their dress, but ingenious, sensible and virtuous. Late travellers, however, have represented them as paying little regard to their moral conduct, and that unnatural crimes were too frequently practiced among them. There is an inveterate enmity between the Choctaws and Creek Indians.

The Creek confederacy forms the largest and most powerful nation of Indians south of the Ohio. The nation with whom the confederacy originated, was called *Muskogulge.* who emigrated from the west, beyond the Mississippi, and established themselves on the ruins of the Natchez. These people made their first settlement on the *Oakmulge Fields,* in the State of Georgia. They gradually subdued their surrounding enemies, and then strengthened themselves by taking into confederacy the vanquished tribes. The principal nations and tribes composing this union, are the Appalachies, Alabamas, Abecas, Cawillaws, Coosas, Conshacks, Coosactees, Chacsihoomas, Natchez, Oconies, Oakmulgies, Okohoys, Pakanas, Taensas, Talepoosas, Weetunkas, and others who have since been united with them. This confederation has rendered them formidable to all the nations around them, as well as to the white people, and has rendered them victorious over the Chickasaws. They are divided into Upper Creeks, and Middle and Lower Creeks. The Upper Creeks include all the waters of the Koose, Talepoose and Alabama rivers, and are called *Abbaco.* Their hunting ground extends to the Tombigby river, which is the dividing line between the Creeks and Chocktaws. The Middle Creeks include all the waters of the Chattahoose and Flint rivers, down to their junction, and although occupied by a great number of different tribes, the whole are called *Ooweta* people, from the Cowetan town and tribe, the most warlike, and one of the most ancient of the Creek nation. The Lower Creeks take in the Appalachicola river, and extend to the point of East Florida. This division is called the *Seminoles.* They have fifty-five principal towns, besides many villages. The smallest towns have from twenty to thirty, and some of the largest from one hundred and fifty to two hundred houses. The towns are all built compact. The houses stand in clusters of 4, 5, 6, 7 and 8 together, irregularly arranged up and down the banks of the rivers and small streams. Each cluster contains a clan, or family of relations, who eat and live in common. Each town has a public square, hot-house and yard near the centre, appropriated to various public uses. General M'Gillivra, estimated the number of warriors to be about six thousand exclusive of the Seminoles, who are considered of little account in war. From their roving manner of living it is impossible to ascertain the number of Creek Indians with much precision. They probably may have about 26,000 souls.

The land which thay claim as their country is a common stock; and any individual may remove from one part of it to another, and occupy vacant ground where he can find it. They have considered their boundary northward, to be some where about the forty-second degree of north latitude (as it has been found by surveyers), extending westward to the Tombigby river, and eastward to the atlantic ocean ; but they have ceded parts of this tract on the sea coast, long ago, by different treaties to the State of Georgia. Their country is hilly, but not mountainous; the soil fertile ; abounding with creeks, from whence they are probably called the Creek Indians. They have been very desirous to agree with the United States on a permanent boundary line, over which the southern States should not trespass. In August 1790, the United States concluded a treaty with the Kings, chiefs and warriors, of the Creek nation, at New-York. By this treaty the boundary line was to begin where the old line strikes the River Savannah; thence up the river to a place called Keowee, where a northeast line to be drawn from the top of the Occunna mountain shall intersect; thence along the said line in a southwest direction, to Tugelo river; thence to the top of the Currahee mountain ; thence to the head or source of the main south branch of the Oconee river, called the Appalachee ; thence down the said branch and River Oconee, to its confluence with the Oakmulgee, which form the River Altamaha to the old line, and thence along the old line to the River Saint Mary. The United States were, from time to time, to furnish the Creek nation gratuitously with useful domestic animals and implements of husbandry. A subsequent treaty was concluded, at Colerain, in June 1796, confirming the former treaty, providing that the boundary line from the Currahee mountain, should be clearly ascertained and marked, and stipulating to give to the said nation, goods to the value of 6,000 dollars, and to send two black smiths, with strikers and necessary tools, to be employed for the Upper and Lower Creeks.

Considerable improvements have been made by these people in agriculture, but they have been extremely deficient in their implements of husbandry. A very large part of the nation being devoted to hunting in the winter, and to war or idleness in the summer, they cultivate only small tracts of land which are barely sufficient to afford them sustenance. Some, who possess numbers of negroes, have fenced fields; but having no ploughs, they are obliged to break up, and cultivate the ground with hoes. The seed is scattered over the ground promiscuously, and not planted in rows. The articles they cultivate, are tobacco, rice, Indian corn, potatoes, beans, peas, cabbage and melons. Such fruits as peaches, plumbs, grapes, and strawberries, they have in great plenty. They raise great numbers of horses, cattle and hogs, and abound in turkies, ducks and other poultry. They manufacture earthern pots and pans, baskets, horse ropes or halters, smoaked leather, black marble pipes, wooden spoons, and oil from acorns, hickory nuts and chesnuts.

The Creeks are not disposed to have much intercourse with white people, especially foreigners, except with the English. Their prejudice is strong in favour of that nation, and they still believe "the Great King over the water" is able to keep the whole world in subjection. They have a particular fondness for British guns, drums, and other articles manufactured by the English people.

It is said the *Muskogulge* language, which is soft and musical, is spoken throughout the confederacy, although different tribes retain their native tongues. These people are generally well formed, expert, hardy, sagacious and politic. They are extremely jealous of their rights, and averse to parting with their lands. They are faithful friends, but inveterate enemies ; hospitable to strangers ; and honest and fair in their dealings. They have a most contemptable opinion of the white man's faith, and yet place great confidence in the justice and integrity of the government of the United States. They have no coercive laws, but support an excellent policy in their civil government. It is said some of their most favourite songs and dances, they have received from their enemies, the Choctaws, who are distinguished for poetry and music. They allow polygamy in the greatest latitude. Any man may take as many wives as he pleases, but the first wife is to be treated as queen, and the rest as only hand-maids and associates. One of the regulations said to have been adopted by the Creek nation, merits the highest commendation. It is the prohibition of the use of spirituous liquors. In their treaties with the white people, it has been said, they have insisted that no kind of spirits should be sold to their people ; and when attempts have been made to run kegs of spirits, the Indians, on a discovery, have destroyed them with their tomahawks.

The Catalaw nation is only the remnant of a formidable, brave, generous people, now reduced to a small tribe. They reside on a river of the same name, which forms a boundary line between North and South Carolina. In their present situation, they are entirely surrounded by white inhabitants. A tract of land of 444,000 acres, has been assigned them, on which they have agricultural improvements. They are said to consist of about four hundred and fifty souls, and have about one hundred and fifty warriors.

An account has been given of a particular tribe of Indians residing, on elevated land, in a part of the Eokeefanoke, or Ekanfanoga swamp, between Flint and Oakmulgee rivers, from which the River Saint Mary takes its rise. It is called a lake, or rather a marsh, three hundred miles in circumference. The account given of these Indians, borders too much on romance to deserve much credit. The lake or marsh is called Ouaquaphenoga. "In wet seasons it appears like an inland sea, and has several large islands of rich land; one of which the present generation of Creek Indians represent as the most blissful spot on earth. They say it is inhabited by a peculiar race of Indians, whose women are incomparably beautiful. They tell that this terrestrial paradise has been seen by some enterprising hunters, when in pursuit of their game, who being lost in inextricable swamps and bogs, and on the point of perishing, were unexpectedly relieved by a company of beautiful women, whom they call daughters of the sun, who kindly gave them such provisions as they had with them; consisting of fruit and corn cakes, and then enjoined them to fly for safety to their own country, because their husbands were fierce men, and cruel to strangers. They further say, that these hunters had a view of their settlements, situated on the elevated banks of an island, in a beautiful lake; but in all their endeavours to approach it, they were involved in perpetual labyrinths, and, like enchanted land, still as they imagined they had just gained it, it seemed to fly before them; and having quitted the delusive pursuit, they with much difficulty effected their retreat.

"They tell another story concerning this sequestered country, which seems not improbable, which is, that the inhabitants are the posterity of a fugitive remnant of the ancient Yamases, who escaped massacre, after a bloody and decisive battle between them and the Creeks, (who, it is certain, conquered and nearly exterminated that once powerful people), and here formed an asylum, remote and secure from the fury of their proud conquerors. The River Saint Mary and Sitilla, which fall into the Atlantic, and the beautiful Little Juan, which empties into the bay of Appalachi, at Saint Mark's, are said by Bartram, to flow from this lake."[†]

* See *Ouaquaphenogaw, American Gazetteer.*

Mr. Purcell, in his account of the population of the Indian nations south of the Ohio, has stated the number of warriors to be 15,516, which is 1,260 more, than is here given. The number of souls are considerable less, being 42,033, and 2,260 less than the preceding estimation. Although he appears to have taken his numbers from actual enumeration, he makes the proportion of warriors, to the number of souls, only a small fraction more than three souls to one warrior, which is considerably less than the common rule of calculation. It is not improbable, however, that his account is correct. It has been a general opinion that these nations have been increasing in number, for a considerable time past. The greatest enemy to their population has doubtless been the intemperate use of spirituous liquors.

Table of the probable number of warriors and souls of the Indians, residing west of the Allegany mountains and vicinity of the lakes, within the limits of the United States.

Names.	No. Warriors.	Estimated No. of Souls.
NORTH OF THE OHIO.		
Six Nations,	1400	4508
Wyandots,	250	800
Wyandot tribes,	300	1000
Delawares,	600	2000
Shawanoes,	300	900
Ottawas,	900	3000
Chippewas,	1550	4000
Putawatimes,	500	2000
Miamis,	300	1000
Piankoshaws, Kickapoos, Musquitons, Ouiatanos,	1000	3500
Kickapoos, Outtagamies, Musquakeys,	1000	3500
Naudowesies,	500	2000
Killistinoes,	250	800
Mingoes,	50	200
Lezars,	300	1000
Outimaes.	200	700
Winnebagoes,	300	1000
Illinois,	260	1000
SOUTH OF THE OHIO.		
Cherokees,	1500	4000
Chicksaws,	575	1725
Chocktaws.	4041	12128
Creeks,	6000	26000
Catabaws,	150	450
	22,226	77,101

THE END.

The First American Frontier
AN ARNO PRESS/NEW YORK TIMES COLLECTION

Agnew, Daniel.
A History of the Region of Pennsylvania North of the Allegheny River. 1887.

Alden, George H.
New Government West of the Alleghenies Before 1780. 1897.

Barrett, Jay Amos.
Evolution of the Ordinance of 1787. 1891.

Billon, Frederick.
Annals of St. Louis in its Early Days Under the French and Spanish Dominations. 1886.

Billon, Frederick.
Annals of St. Louis in its Territorial Days, 1804-1821. 1888.

Littel, William.
Political Transactions in and Concerning Kentucky. 1926.

Bowles, William Augustus.
Authentic Memoirs of William Augustus Bowles. 1916.

Bradley, A. G.
The Fight with France for North America. 1900.

Brannan, John, ed.
Official Letters of the Military and Naval Officers of the War, 1812-1815. 1823.

Brown, John P.
Old Frontiers. 1938.

Brown, Samuel R.
The Western Gazetteer. 1817.

Cist, Charles.
Cincinnati Miscellany of Antiquities of the West and Pioneer History. (2 volumes in one). 1845-6.

Claiborne, Nathaniel Herbert.
Notes on the War in the South with Biographical Sketches of the Lives of Montgomery, Jackson, Sevier, and Others. 1819.

Clark, Daniel.
Proofs of the Corruption of Gen. James Wilkinson. 1809.

Clark, George Rogers.
Colonel George Rogers Clark's Sketch of His Campaign in the Illinois in 1778-9. 1869.

Collins, Lewis.
Historical Sketches of Kentucky. 1847.

Cruikshank, Ernest, ed,
Documents Relating to Invasion of Canada and the Surrender of Detroit. 1912.

Cruikshank, Ernest, ed,
The Documentary History of the Campaign on the Niagara Frontier, 1812-1814. (4 volumes). 1896-1909.

Cutler, Jervis.
A Topographical Description of the State of Ohio, Indian Territory, and Louisiana. 1812.

Cutler, Julia P.
The Life and Times of Ephraim Cutler. 1890.

Darlington, Mary C.
History of Col. Henry Bouquet and the Western Frontiers of Pennsylvania. 1920.

Darlington, Mary C.
Fort Pitt and Letters From the Frontier. 1892.

De Schweinitz, Edmund.
The Life and Times of David Zeisberger. 1870.

Dillon, John B.
History of Indiana. 1859.

Eaton, John Henry.
Life of Andrew Jackson. 1824.

English, William Hayden.
Conquest of the Country Northwest of the Ohio. (2 volumes in one). 1896.

Flint, Timothy.
Indian Wars of the West. 1833.

Forbes, John.
Writings of General John Forbes Relating to His Service in North America. 1938.

Forman, Samuel S.
Narrative of a Journey Down the Ohio and Mississippi in 1789-90. 1888.

Haywood, John.
Civil and Political History of the State of Tennessee to 1796. 1823.

Heckewelder, John.
History, Manners and Customs of the Indian Nations. 1876.

Heckewelder, John.
Narrative of the Mission of the United Brethren. 1820.

Hildreth, Samuel P.
Pioneer History. 1848.

Houck, Louis.
The Boundaries of the Louisiana Purchase: A Historical Study. 1901.

Houck, Louis.
History of Missouri. (3 volumes in one). 1908.

Houck, Louis.
The Spanish Regime in Missouri. (2 volumes in one). 1909.

Jacob, John J.
A Biographical Sketch of the Life of the Late Capt. Michael Cresap. 1826.

Jones, David.
A Journal of Two Visits Made to Some Nations of Indians on the West Side of the River Ohio, in the Years 1772 and 1773. 1774.

Kenton, Edna.
Simon Kenton. 1930.

Loudon, Archibald.
Selection of Some of the Most Interesting Narratives of Outrages. (2 volumes in one). 1808-1811.

Monette, J. W.
History, Discovery and Settlement of the Mississippi Valley. (2 volumes in one). 1846.

Morse, Jedediah.
American Gazetteer. 1797.

Pickett, Albert James.
History of Alabama. (2 volumes in one). 1851.

Pope, John.
A Tour Through the Southern and Western Territories. 1792.

Putnam, Albigence Waldo.
History of Middle Tennessee. 1859.

Ramsey, James G. M.
Annals of Tennessee. 1853.

Ranck, George W.
Boonesborough. 1901.

Robertson, James Rood, ed.
Petitions of the Early Inhabitants of Kentucky to the Gen. Assembly of Virginia. 1914.

Royce, Charles.
Indian Land Cessions. 1899.

Rupp, I. Daniel.
History of Northampton, Lehigh, Monroe, Carbon and Schuykill Counties. 1845.

Safford, William H.
The Blennerhasset Papers. 1864.

St. Clair, Arthur.
A Narrative of the Manner in which the Campaign Against the Indians, in the Year 1791 was Conducted. 1812.

Sargent, Winthrop, ed.
A History of an Expedition Against Fort DuQuesne in 1755. 1855.

Severance, Frank H.
An Old Frontier of France. (2 volumes in one). 1917.

Sipe, C. Hale.
Fort Ligonier and Its Times. 1932.

Stevens, Henry N.
Lewis Evans: His Map of the Middle British Colonies in America. 1920.

Timberlake, Henry.
The Memoirs of Lieut. Henry Timberlake. 1927.

Tome, Philip.
Pioneer Life: Or Thirty Years a Hunter. 1854.

Trent, William.
Journal of Captain William Trent From Logstown to Pickawillany. 1871.

Walton, Joseph S.
Conrad Weiser and the Indian Policy of Colonial Pennsylvania. 1900.

Withers, Alexander Scott.
Chronicles of Border Warfare. 1895.